Canada

Canada

BY LIZ SONNEBORN

Enchantment of the World™
Second Series

Children's Press®

An Imprint of Scholastic Inc.

NEW YORK   TORONTO   LONDON   AUCKLAND   SYDNEY
MEXICO CITY   NEW DELHI   HONG KONG
DANBURY, CONNECTICUT

Frontispiece: Totem pole and provincial parliament building in Victoria, British Columbia

Consultant: Anthony B. Chan, PhD, is professor and founding associate dean of the Communication Program at the University of Ontario Institute of Technology, Oshawa, Ontario. Before returning to Canada, he was Director of Canadian Studies at the University of Washington and Principal Investigator of the National Resource Center for the Study of Canada supported by the Department of Education, Washington, D.C.

Please note: All statistics are as up-to-date as possible at the time of publication.

Book production by The Design Lab

Library of Congress Cataloging-in-Publication Data

Sonneborn, Liz.
  Canada/by Liz Sonneborn.
      p. cm.—(Enchantment of the world. Second series)
  Includes bibliographical references and index.
  ISBN-13: 978-0-531-25351-9 (lib. bdg.)
  ISBN-10: 0-531-25351-1 (lib. bdg.)
  1. Canada—Juvenile literature. I. Title. II. Series.
  F1008.2.S66 2012
  971—dc22   2011011970

SCHOLASTIC, CHILDREN'S PRESS, and associated logos are trademarks and/or registered trademarks of Scholastic Inc.
1 2 3 4 5 6 7 8 9 10 R 21 20 19 18 17 16 15 14 13 12

Canada

Contents

Cover photo:
Canadian
Mounted Police

Kayaking on
Hudson Bay

Newfoundland dog

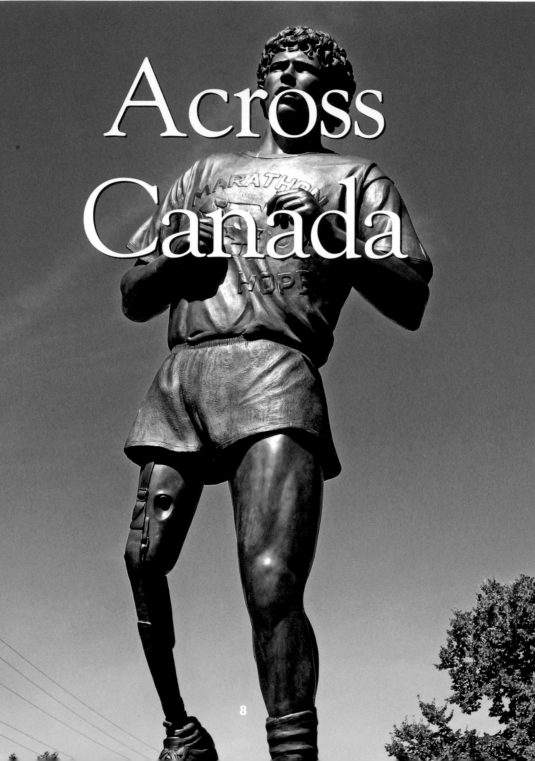

Across Canada

ON APRIL 12, 1980, TERRY FOX STOOD ON A BEACH, preparing to take part in a great journey. He filled two jars with water from the Atlantic Ocean. One he was going to keep as a souvenir. The other he planned to empty into the Pacific Ocean at the end of his adventure. Fox was about to begin a run from ocean to ocean, all the way across Canada.

The plan was ambitious. After all, Canada is the second-largest nation in the world. Only Russia, in Asia, is bigger. From its easternmost point to its westernmost point, Canada measures a whopping 3,426 miles (5,514 kilometers). But because he would have to run along winding roadways, Fox's planned trip would be far longer.

Even though Fox had trained long and hard for his run, the challenge he set for himself was extreme. Three years before, Fox had lost most of his right leg to cancer. He would be running on his one good leg and on an artificial limb. After he filled his jars with water, he placed his artificial foot into the cool Atlantic, looking forward to the day he could do the same in the Pacific, though the dream was still a country's width away.

Opposite: **This statue of Terry Fox, a great Canadian hero, stands in Victoria, British Columbia. There are statues of him all across Canada.**

CANADA

- Cities of over 50,000 people
- Smaller cities and towns
- Department capitals

0   400 miles

0   600 kilometers

ARCTIC OCEAN

Alaska

Sverdrup Is.

Queen Elizabeth Islands

Resolute • Cornwallis I.

Baffin Island

Greenland

Yukon Territory

Great Bear Lake

Fort Franklin

Northwest Territories

Nunavut

Iqaluit

Labrador Sea

Whitehorse

Great Slave Lake

Yellowknife

Queen Charlotte Is.

L. Athabasca

Hudson Bay

Churchill

NEWFOUNDLAND

BRITISH COLUMBIA

ALBERTA

SASKATCHEWAN

MANITOBA

QUEBEC

Gander

Prince George

St. John's

Jasper

Edmonton

L. Louise

Vancouver I.

Kamloops

Banff

Calgary

L. Winnipeg

ONTARIO

Gulf of St. Lawrence

C. St. Mary's

Vancouver

Regina

NEW BRUNSWICK

Charlottetown

C. Breton I.

Victoria

Winnipeg

Quebec

Saint John

PRINCE EDWARD ISLAND

L. Superior

Sudbury

Montreal

Halifax

Sault Ste. Marie

Ottawa

L. Champlain

NOVA SCOTIA

UNITED STATES

L. Huron

Toronto

Kingston

L. Michigan

Hamilton

London

L. Ontario

ATLANTIC OCEAN

Windsor

Niagara Falls

L. Erie

Canada

A Devastating Diagnosis

Until his diagnosis, Fox had led a fairly uneventful life. Born on July 28, 1958, he was raised in the Canadian province of British Columbia. (Canada is made up of thirteen divisions, similar to states in the United States. Ten are called provinces;

three are called territories.) Fox loved playing sports and hoped someday to become a physical education teacher.

During his first year in college, he felt a pain in his right knee but ignored it. Then one day, he could not stand. On March 9, 1977, Fox's doctor told him terrible news. Fox had a rare form of blood cancer. A tumor was causing the pain in his leg. The only way to save Fox's life was to amputate (cut off) his leg just above the knee. The night before his surgery, Fox read an article about Dick Traum, the first amputee ever to complete the New York Marathon, a race that covers 26 miles (42 km). Traum's story gave Fox hope that he could still do great things with his life.

Even after his successful recovery, Fox could not shake memories of the cancer ward of his hospital. He was upset by the suffering of fellow cancer patients and inspired by their

Terry Fox grew up in Port Coquitlam, British Columbia, on the west coast of Canada.

courage. Fox was also angry. He felt that Canada was not providing enough funds to medical research for finding a cure for cancer. Fox decided to do something about it.

The Marathon of Hope

Fox was determined to run across Canada to raise money for cancer research. He called his idea the Marathon of Hope.

The twenty-one-year-old Fox began his run in the city of St. John's, Newfoundland. Within days, Fox was bullied by harsh winds, freezing rain, and even snow. Still he kept up the pace, trying to run the distance of a marathon each day. Running with an artificial leg gave him an awkward gait. He would make two hops on his left leg and then swing his artificial leg forward. The stump of his right leg was bruised and battered by each step Fox made.

Terry Fox ran across Canada for 143 days.

Word spread about Fox's project. By the time Fox entered Ontario, Canada's most populous province, he was becoming a celebrity. People came out on the street to cheer him on. In Ottawa, the nation's capital, Fox shook the hand of Prime Minister Pierre Trudeau, the most powerful person in the Canadian government. But he was even more excited to meet Bobby Orr, a legendary Canadian hockey player and one of Fox's idols. Orr presented him with a check for $25,000 for cancer research.

Canada's embrace of the Marathon of Hope buoyed Fox. But then, on September 1, Fox began to feel a great pain in his chest and began to cough uncontrollably. He tried resting, and he tried running through the pain, but there was no relief. He had to go to the hospital. He soon learned that cancer had struck his lungs. He had no choice but to quit his run. He had traveled 3,339 miles (5,374 km) over 143 days.

Terry Fox talks with hockey great Bobby Orr. Orr is considered one of the greatest hockey players of all time.

Terry Fox greeted supporters in Toronto. By this time, he had already been running for three months.

A Canadian Hero

Terry Fox died on June 28, 1981, one month shy of his twenty-third birthday. His funeral was broadcast on national television. Prime Minister Trudeau delivered an address on Fox's passing: "It occurs very rarely in the life of a nation that the courageous spirit of one person unites all people in the celebration of his life and in the mourning of his death."

The annual Terry Fox Run is now held in sixty countries each September. The world's largest one-day fund-raiser for cancer, this run has raised more than $550 million. In 2004, a survey named Fox the second-greatest Canadian of all time.

Why did Terry Fox become such a national hero? The answer is rooted in how Canadians see themselves and their history. Canadians embrace Fox because he seems to represent what they regard as their own best qualities.

During his lifetime, Terry Fox shook off the title of hero. The real heroes, he said, were those fighting for their lives every day in cancer hospitals. This kind of modesty is often valued by Canadians. The world over, they are known for being gracious and polite.

About 2.5 million people around the world take part in the Terry Fox Run each year.

Canadians come from a wide variety of ethnic backgrounds.

Fox's desire to help others, even at the expense of his own health, also endears him to Canadians. On a personal level, most Canadians try to get along with those around them and help those who are in need. On a national level, the government of Canada also promotes respect, tolerance, and equality for all its people—no matter their race, religion, or ethnicity. Canadian society is one of the most multicultural in the world, with people of all backgrounds living alongside one another with little conflict. The Canadian government, with the support of most Canadians, also offers generous social programs to help those who are ill or need money.

Canadians' love for Terry Fox also springs from his outsized ambitions. When he was planning his run, many people tried to talk him out of it. Instead of listening to them, Fox kept setting his goals higher, no matter how crazy his ideas sounded to others. Fox achieved far more than anyone imagined he would.

Just like the story of Terry Fox, the story of Canada is about making the seemingly impossible possible. Canada encompasses a huge amount of land, much of it so rugged and harsh that few people live there. But throughout Canadian history, its people boldly delved into the great project of molding Canada into one of the most prosperous nations in the world. It is no wonder that when Canadians look admiringly at the determination and fearlessness of Terry Fox, they are also seeing a little of themselves.

The highway outside of Thunder Bay, Ontario, is named after Terry Fox. Fox was in Thunder Bay when cancer forced him to quit his run.

CHAPTER

TWO

Sea to Sea

18

THE OFFICIAL MOTTO OF CANADA IS *A MARI USQUE AD mare*, "from sea to sea" in the Latin language. The phrase is an apt one to describe the country. From east to west, Canada sits between two great bodies of water, the Atlantic Ocean and the Pacific Ocean. Canada is about 3,400 miles (5,500 km) across and is nearly as tall as it is wide. A line drawn from its northernmost point in the Arctic Ocean to its southernmost point along the U.S. border would measure about 3,000 miles (4,800 km).

Canada is the biggest country in North America. It is made up of all the land north of the United States, except for Alaska and three islands. (The vast island of Greenland belongs to Denmark, while Saint-Pierre and Miquelon belong to France.) Canada has two international boundaries, but both are with the same country—the United States. Its border with the American mainland is 3,987 miles (6,416 km) long. Its border with the state of Alaska measures 1,539 miles (2,477 km).

In a country so large, it is hardly surprising that Canada's land varies greatly from place to place. Depending on where you are, you might see great rivers, rolling hills, flat prairies, majestic mountains, soggy rain forests, or enormous freshwater lakes.

Opposite. **Cape Breton Highlands National Park in Nova Scotia boasts steep cliffs and pounding waves.**

Canada's Geographic Features

Area: 3,855,102 square miles (9,984,668 sq km)

Length of border: 5,526 miles (8,893 km) with the United States

Length of coastline: 125,567 miles (202,081 km)

Highest elevation: 19,551 feet (5,959 m), at Mount Logan

Lowest elevation: Sea level, along the coasts

Largest island: Baffin Island, 195,927 square miles (507,449 sq km)

Longest river: Mackenzie River, 2,635 miles (4,241 km)

Largest lake: Lake Superior, 31,700 square miles (82,100 sq km); 11,100 square miles (28,700 sq km) in Canada

Highest waterfall: Della Falls, 1,444 feet (440 m) drop

City with hottest average summer temperatures: Kamloops, British Columbia, 80°F (27°C)

City with the coldest average winter temperatures: Yellowknife, Northwest Territories, −22°F (−30°C)

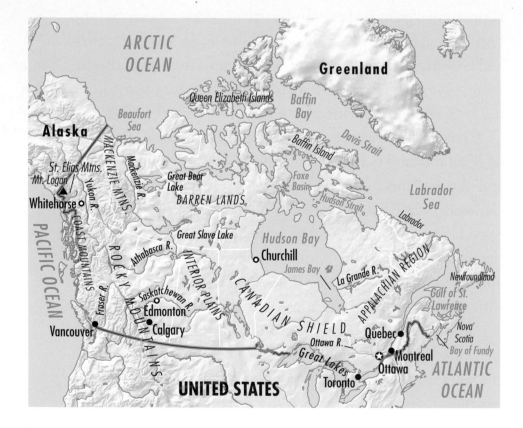

The Appalachian Region and the Canadian Shield

Geographers call the hilly, forested area of southeastern Canada the Appalachian Region. It includes the provinces of Newfoundland and Labrador, Prince Edward Island, New Brunswick, and Nova Scotia, as well as the Gaspé Peninsula of Quebec. Also found in the region are the northern reaches of the Appalachian Mountain chain, which stretches through the eastern United States.

The islands in this area feature rocky, craggy coastlines. The coast of New Brunswick along the Bay of Fundy is pounded by some of the most powerful waves in the world. The Appalachian Region's cold winds and rugged terrain make it a difficult place to live, so the population is fairly small.

Gros Morne National Park in Newfoundland is part of the Long Range Mountains, the northernmost section of the Appalachian range.

The Canadian Shield typically features a lot of pine trees, lakes, and exposed rock.

To the west is a region called the Canadian Shield. This area, which covers about half of Canada, forms a ring around Hudson Bay. Its wild and remote lands include hills, forests, lakes, and swamps.

Interior Plains and Lowlands

A much more hospitable area is the Great Lakes-St. Lawrence Lowlands of southern Ontario and Quebec. The cities of Toronto, Montreal, Ottawa, and Quebec City are found in the lowlands. Throughout Canada's history, the area has been the leading center for farming and industry.

Looking at Canada's Cities

Toronto, the capital city of Ontario, is Canada's largest city. The city proper has about 2.5 million people, but the larger metropolitan area is home to more than double that number. Toronto is probably the most ethnically diverse city in the world. As a major job center, it attracts many immigrants. In fact, nearly half of its population was born outside of Canada. Toronto is the country's financial center. Most of Canada's largest banking, insurance, communications, and financial services companies are headquartered in Toronto. The city skyline is dominated by the CN Tower (below), a telecommunications spire that has become a symbol of the city. Toronto is also the cultural capital of English-speaking Canada. One of the city's highlights is the Royal Ontario Museum, which features exhibits on nature and human culture from around the world.

Located in southeastern Quebec, Montreal is Canada's second-largest city with about 1.6 million people. Montreal is the center of French-speaking culture in North America. Most of its residents count French as their first language. The city sits on an island, Île de Montréal, where the St. Lawrence and Ottawa rivers meet. An excellent port for shipping, Montreal has long been a major industrial center. The city has a diverse population. Some groups, such as people with Jewish or Chinese backgrounds, have a long history in Montreal. Others, such as Haitians and Greeks, only recently began immigrating to Montreal in large numbers. Montreal offers an exciting cultural scene, with many theaters, museums, art galleries, and music venues. Each July, jazz fans from the world over arrive for the Montreal International Jazz Festival.

Calgary, Alberta, is the third-largest city in Canada with nearly 1 million people. Calgary sits on the western edge of the interior plains. The city began as a fort in 1875. After the railroad came through in 1883, it became a center for processing and shipping agricultural products, such as wheat and beef. In the twentieth century, oil was discovered nearby, and Calgary remains a center of the Canadian oil industry. Calgary is proud of its western heritage, and each year it holds the Calgary Stampede, a rodeo and celebration of western life. In 1988, Calgary hosted the Winter Olympics. Today, Calgary Olympic Park, where many of the Olympic events were held, is a popular site for skiing, snowboarding, and sledding. In summer, mountain bikers hit the slopes.

The Saint Elias Range boasts the five highest mountains in Canada. Many peaks in the range top 17,000 feet (5,200 m).

Another region known for agriculture is the interior plains, which spread across Manitoba, Saskatchewan, and Alberta. The area is an extension of the Great Plains of the central United States. It features excellent farmland, especially for growing wheat and other grains. The plains area is also rich in natural resources, such as oil and natural gas. The region's leading cities include Winnipeg, Manitoba; Saskatoon and Regina, Saskatchewan; and Calgary and Edmonton, Alberta.

The Cordillera Region and the Arctic Archipelago

To the west is the Cordillera Region, which extends to the Pacific Coast. Including portions of Alberta and most of British Columbia and Yukon Territory, it features a series of mountain ranges, including the Rocky, Coast, and Saint Elias Mountains. Mount Logan, which, at 19,551 feet (5,959 meters), is the highest point in all of Canada, rises in the Saint Elias Range. Located in the Pacific Ocean, Vancouver Island and the Queen Charlotte Islands, or Haida Gwaii (Islands of the People), are peaks in an underwater mountain range.

Far to the north is Canada's Arctic region. This area is so cold and dry that the top layer of soil is permanently frozen. The Arctic includes dramatic ice-covered hills and peaks. It also features an archipelago, or chain of islands. The enormous Baffin

Exploring Canada

Many Canadian geographical sites are named after European explorers.

Baffin Island: In the early nineteenth century, British explorer William Edward Parry led a series of expeditions into the Arctic Ocean. He named the biggest island he found there Baffin Island (right), after William Baffin, another British explorer who had sailed to Canada two hundred years earlier.

Hudson Bay: Hudson Bay is a large body of water in northeastern Canada. It is named after Henry Hudson, the British explorer who first sailed into the bay in his ship, the *Discovery*, in 1610. Fearing for their lives on the dangerous journey, his unhappy crewmen rose up against him and set him adrift in a boat. No one knows for sure what happened to Hudson.

Mackenzie River: The longest river in Canada, the Mackenzie, got its name from Scottish-born Alexander Mackenzie. In 1789, he headed an expedition in search of a river that would provide a travel route to the Pacific Ocean. He thought the Mackenzie was that river, but he soon discovered that it emptied into the Arctic Ocean. After his failed expedition, he called the waterway that now bears his name Disappointment River.

A boy jumps into Lake Huron at Bruce Peninsula National Park in Ontario.

Island is the largest island in Canada and the fifth largest in the world. The Canadian Arctic remains the homeland of the descendants of some of the first people in the region—the Inuits. The weather in much of this region is so punishing that large areas are virtually unpopulated.

Bodies of Water

The lands of Canada are vast and varied. So are the waters within its borders. From lakes to rivers to bays, Canada has a total of 334,080 square miles (865,263 sq km) of water. That area is more than twice the size of the state of California. With its many islands, it also has an enormous length of coastline. You could wrap a string the length of Canada's coastline around the globe twice.

The Great Lakes, the largest group of freshwater lakes in the world, rest on Canada's southern border with the United States. Four of the Great Lakes—Superior, Huron, Erie, and Ontario—lie partly in Canada. The fifth—Lake Michigan—is considered American territory.

Another important body of water in Canada is Hudson Bay, the largest inland sea in the world. On the Canadian map, the outline of Hudson Bay makes it look as though someone took an enormous bite out of northeastern Canada.

Canada's longest river is the Mackenzie. Stretching more than 2,635 miles (4,241 km), it flows north from Great Slave Lake in the Northwest Territories to the Arctic Ocean. Other large river systems include the Yukon and the Fraser. The country's most important river, though, is the St. Lawrence. Throughout its history, the St. Lawrence has provided a route from the Atlantic Ocean to the rich lands in the interior. The river's use as a trading route became even more important after the opening of the St. Lawrence Seaway in 1959. This waterway was built to extend the St. Lawrence, thereby allowing large ships to travel from the Atlantic Ocean to the Great Lakes.

An Inuit man steers a kayak across Hudson Bay. The area around Hudson Bay is so cold that there are only about a dozen communities along its shore.

A Varied Climate

The Great White North is a nickname for Canada commonly used both inside and outside its borders. But, contrary to the name, all of Canada is not always covered with a blanket of snow. Like so much about Canada, the real story is more complicated. The climate of Canada varies a great deal depending on the time of year and location.

For much of the year, the weather in southern Quebec and Ontario is fairly comfortable. Not surprisingly, this is the region where most Canadians live. For instance, summer in Toronto, Ontario, is warm, with highs averaging about 80 degrees Fahrenheit (27 degrees Celsius) in July. Usually, for a few weeks in summer, the heat and humidity are so high the air is stifling. But, before and after such a heat wave, the Toronto summer is known for its warm days and cool nights.

The winter, though, is another story. The moist air produces a great deal of snow. Toronto gets an average of 52 inches (132 centimeters) of snow a year. Farther to the north and east, the annual snowfall is usually much more.

The interior plains have the most extreme weather in Canada. In the short summer, the area is often very dry and very hot, with temperatures sometimes soaring above 100°F (38°C). Its long winter is not as snowy as in the East, yet the plains are frequently bitterly cold. The winter chill, however, is relieved by chinook winds. In about one of every three winter days, these warming winds flow down the eastern slope of the Rocky Mountains into southwestern Alberta. An extreme chinook can raise the temperature of the region by as much as 35°F (20°C).

The most temperate area of Canada is found west of the Rockies along the Pacific coast. In coastal British Columbia, both winters and summers are mild. The mountains of the Cordillera protect the area from cold Arctic air. At the same time, because of winds from the west, British Columbia can be moist and humid. For much of the winter, heavy rains make the region dark, dank, and dreary. Mainland British Columbia gets rainfall of about 60 inches (150 cm) a year, while as much as 100 inches (250 cm) falls on Vancouver Island.

Canada's harshest weather occurs in the Arctic. There, a blanket of snow covers the ground for at least ten months of the year. While Canada as a whole is no Great White North, this is a fair description of its northernmost region.

The Living World

With its enormous size, Canada is blessed with a wide array of plants and animals. The magnificent natural world has helped shape Canada's national identity. A love of nature is a large part of what defines Canadians.

Forests Everywhere

Perhaps Canada's greatest natural resource is its forests. Almost half of Canada is covered with trees.

Some 150 species of trees grow in Canada. Eastern Canada is full of beeches, pines, and maples. In addition to being a national symbol, the maple provides maple syrup, a delicious treat many Canadians love. South of the Arctic, common trees include white birch and spruce. The far western forests are known for their red cedars and Douglas firs.

Trees are harvested for lumber all over Canada. But forests of Douglas fir, which cover much of British Columbia, are a particularly rich source of timber. The area boasts the oldest living fir tree, thought to be about 1,300 years old.

The Mighty Maple

Because of its role in the country's history, culture, and economy, the maple is Canada's national tree. Great forests of maple trees have long provided Canadians with delicious syrup and with wood used to build homes and furniture. Selling wood products to other countries has helped the Canadian economy. In addition to the tree's practical uses, Canadians celebrate the beauty of their vast maple tree forests. A bright red maple leaf appears in the center of the Canadian flag.

Plant Life

Besides trees, many other plants thrive in the Canadian wilderness. About three thousand species were native to Canada before Europeans first arrived there. Since then, thousands of species from other areas of the world have been introduced to Canadian lands.

A mixture of grasses grows wild on the interior plains. But because of the fertile soil there, large portions of these grasslands have been cleared to make room for farms and ranches. The region is now covered by fields of wheat, barley, and other crops, or by grazing lands for cattle and other livestock.

Far to the north, in the dry and frozen Arctic, no trees can survive. But some especially hardy plants do manage to grow. They include mosses, small bushes, grasses, and lichens (slow-growing plants that attach themselves to rocks).

When monarch butterflies are migrating, they travel up to 45 miles (75 km) a day.

Bugs, Butterflies, and Birds

Canada is home to many different species of animals, small and large. The greatest variety of creatures in Canada is found among insects. About fifty-five thousand species have been identified. But there are likely to be about thirty thousand more in remote and uncharted areas of the north. Among the best-known insects in Canada is the monarch butterfly. During autumn in southwestern Ontario, thousands of these orange and black butterflies can be spied as they begin their annual migration south.

Among the dozens of amphibians and reptiles commonly found in Canada are painted turtles, spotted salamanders, and western rattlesnakes. The moderate temperatures of the St. Lawrence Lowlands and British Columbia are particularly attractive to these animals. These creatures are rare in Canada's

Lovely Loons

Known for its beautiful call, the common loon is Canada's national bird. An image of a loon appears on the Canadian dollar coin, which is appropriately nicknamed the loonie.

northern reaches because they are cold-blooded and therefore require the warmth of the sun to heat their bodies. No snakes live in Yukon, Nunavut, or Newfoundland and Labrador.

Because of its wetlands, Canada is a paradise for birds. Common waterbirds include the Canada goose, the mallard duck, and the great blue heron. One of the most charming native birds is the Atlantic puffin. Colored black and white

The Canada Goose

The Canada goose is a large waterfowl easily identified by its distinctive black head and neck and the strip of white across its chin. During the warmer months, large flocks of Canada geese can be found in much of Canada. As the weather turns cold, the geese start off on their annual migration south. Flying in a V formation, they head to more temperate areas in the United States to spend the winter. Come spring, most return to the northern United States and Canada for mating season. Canada geese are among the few animals that mate for life. They are also very protective parents. Geese families often swim in a straight row, with the mother at one end and the father at the other so they can better look after their offspring.

with orange beaks, these little birds walk on land in an awkward waddle. They are fine swimmers, however. Able to hold their breath underwater for more than a minute, they feed on small fish. In one dive, puffins are often able to catch ten or more fish in their beaks.

Canada's largest bird is the bald eagle. From tip to tip, this eagle's full wingspan can be as long as 96 inches (244 cm). These impressive creatures live throughout southern Canada, but their preferred habitat is the Pacific coastal region.

Puffins live in large colonies. More than a quarter of a million pairs of puffins live at Witless Bay Ecological Reserve, south of St. John's, Newfoundland.

From the Sea

With its lengthy coastline, Canada is naturally rich in fish species. Its coastal waters are home to cod, halibut, and salmon, while its rivers and freshwater lakes teem with carp, trout, and pike.

Whales frequent Canada's waters on both coasts. Off the shores of New Brunswick and Nova Scotia, whale watchers may see several species, from the small beluga to the blue whale, the largest animal on the planet. From Vancouver Island, they may spy a black-and-white orca swimming in the Pacific. Orcas, also called killer whales, feed on seals and other whales. They swim through the water with astonishing speed, moving as fast as 25 miles per hour (40 kph).

Woolly Wildlife

The wilds of Canada make happy homes for many different fur-bearing animals. None is more closely associated with the country than the beaver. Beavers live in forests throughout the country. Their muscular tails help them navigate Canada's many lakes and rivers. As they swim, their tails help steer them in the right direction.

Orcas are frequently seen off the coast of British Columbia. They sometimes leap out of the water playfully.

The Beaver

Canada's national animal is the beaver. It might seem strange to embrace the largest rodent in North America as a national symbol, but Canadians know they owe a great deal to the beaver. The first French and British settlers came to what is now Canada because of the beaver fur trade. In this way, the beaver was vital to the early settlement of Canada. The country honors its debt to the beaver by featuring it on the Canadian five-cent coin.

Other common small mammals in Canada include the flying squirrel, the porcupine, and the snowshoe hare. The flying squirrel does not really fly. It has a membrane connecting its wrists and ankles that allows it to glide through the air as it jumps from tree to tree. The porcupine is known for its sharp quills, which protect it from predators. In Canada, native craftspeople have long used dyed porcupine quills to create colorful patterns on clothing, bags, and boxes made from birchbark. The snowshoe hare is named for its large feet, which allow it to walk on snow without sinking. During the snowy winter, the snowshoe hare's brown fur turns white to help it hide from predators.

The greatest threat to the snowshoe hare is the Canadian lynx. Lynx have short bodies, long legs, and triangle-shaped ears with little tufts of fur on the tips. Lynx are not fast animals. To catch hares, they patiently lie in wait, prepared to make a surprise pounce on a hare unlucky enough to scamper by.

Elk are much larger than deer. Males stand about 5 feet (1.5 m) high at the shoulder.

Another feared predator is the wolf. Wolves will often attack prey far larger than themselves, including moose. Moose are most commonly found in Canada's western mountain ranges. Their long legs help them travel easily, even in deep snow. Western Canada is also home to herds of elk, a species of large deer. The smaller white-tailed deer can be found in forests across the country.

Black bears are also common in Canada's forests. Their fearsome cousin, the grizzly, is found in mountainous areas. The Arctic north is the perfect environment for polar bears. About half of the polar bears in the world live in the Canadian territory of Nunavut.

Other Arctic animals include caribou and reindeer. These animals feed on moss and lichen. The arctic fox is built well for extremely cold temperatures. It has fur on the bottom of its feet to protect them from snow and ice. The fox's pelt is one of the thickest of any animal. Its fur is so warm that an arctic fox can feel comfortable in temperatures as low as –60°F (–50°C).

Protecting Canada's Wildlands

Most Canadians live in urban areas rather than wildlands, but they have plenty of opportunities to see native animals. A few small animals—such as mice, pigeons, raccoons, skunks, and squirrels—live side by side with humans in even the most densely populated areas. To see larger and rarer animals in their natural habitats, city dwellers visit parks and reserves that have been established to provide animals a safe place to live.

Polar bear cubs typically stay with their mothers for about two and a half years.

Visitors stroll on a boardwalk through the marshes at Point Pelee National Park, giving them a good view of wildlife.

Animals face many threats. The population of Canada grew quickly in the last century. Areas where animals once roamed free were overtaken by human settlement. Some animals, such as the black-footed ferret, the sea otter, and the right whale, were hunted almost to extinction. The populations of the peregrine falcon and the Atlantic salmon dwindled because of pollution. Many creatures could no longer survive in waters that people used for recreation, such as swimming and motorboating.

One safe place for animals is the Witless Bay Ecological Reserve in Newfoundland. It protects seabirds and other marine life. The reserve is a popular center for whale watching. For bird lovers, Point Pelee National Park in Ontario is a favorite spot. The park is a stopping point for songbirds and butterflies on their annual migrations. And, since 1922, the Wood Buffalo National Park, located in Alberta and the Northwest Territories, has provided visitors with the opportunity to see one of Canada's mightiest creatures—the bison, commonly known as the buffalo. Because of overhunting, the bison was once nearly extinct. But through careful preservation efforts, a herd of about five thousand now roams the park, safe and free.

Newfoundlands and Labradors

When dog lovers hear the words *Newfoundland and Labrador*, they are less likely to think of the Canadian province than of two breeds of big, powerful dogs. Both breeds are native to Canada.

Often called gentle giants, Newfoundlands (left) weigh about 100 to 150 pounds (45 to 68 kilograms). Despite their heavy, woolly coats, they are excellent swimmers. There are several cases on record of Newfoundlands helping to save humans from drowning.

Generally smaller and leaner than Newfoundlands, Labradors have a short coat. Because of their friendly natures, they are good family pets and are one of the most popular dog breeds in Canada and the United States. Many Labradors have been successfully trained as guide dogs to help the blind.

CHAPTER

FOUR

Making History

IN 1497, THE ITALIAN EXPLORER GIOVANNI CABOTO, ALSO known as John Cabot, obtained backing from the English king Henry VII for an expedition. Leaving Bristol, England, Cabot and his crew sailed west across the Atlantic Ocean. On June 24, they landed along the eastern coast of what is now Canada. Although Cabot mistakenly believed he had reached Asia, he is now often hailed as the man who "discovered" Canada.

Cabot was not the first foreigner to see Canada's shores, however. Some five hundred years before his voyage, Leif Eriksson and his crew of Norsemen, commonly called Vikings, sailed from Greenland to Canada. In the 1960s, the ruins of a Viking settlement were discovered in L'Anse aux Meadows, Newfoundland.

Yet, Eriksson is no more the discoverer of Canada than John Cabot. That title belongs to the hunters who first crossed from Asia into North America. Sometime around twelve thousand years ago, they likely followed herds of animals across a land bridge where a body of water called the Bering Strait is now located. Eventually, early North Americans

Opposite: **Hunters from Asia crossed the Bering Strait into North America at least twelve thousand years ago.**

moved south and east into what is now Canada. The descendants of these hunters are now referred to as the First Nations people. (These groups are called American Indians or Native Americans in the United States.) A later migration brought the ancestors of another native group to Canada. They are now known as the Inuits.

The French Arrive

Several decades after Cabot's expedition, European exploration of Canada began in earnest. Financed by King Francis I, French explorer Jacques Cartier sailed into the Gulf of St. Lawrence and claimed the surrounding area for France

Jacques Cartier wanted to find a water route through North America to the Pacific. While searching for this route, he became the first European to sail up the St. Lawrence River.

in 1534. French claims in North America were called Nouvelle-France, or New France. But in his diaries, Cartier gave the St. Lawrence region another name—Kanata. It was a word native Huron and Iroquois people used to mean "village." Over time, "Kanata" became "Canada."

Samuel de Champlain established the first permanent French settlement in Canada in 1608. This was just one year after British colonists founded Jamestown, Virginia, the

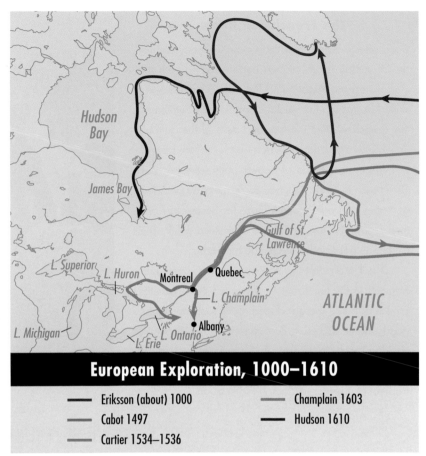

European Exploration, 1000–1610

— Eriksson (about) 1000
— Cabot 1497
— Cartier 1534–1536
— Champlain 1603
— Hudson 1610

first permanent British settlement in North America. Champlain's settlement was located at the Iroquois village of Stadacona, on the cliffs overlooking the St. Lawrence River. Quebec City, one of the oldest cities in Canada, now stands on the site.

During the seventeenth century, another group of French settlers came to Canada. Settling in what is now Nova Scotia and New Brunswick, they survived by fishing and farming the region's fertile lands. These French colonists became known as Acadians, and their land was called Acadia.

The French Fur Trade

Soon after arriving in what is now Canada, Samuel de Champlain and his men began trading with the Huron and the Algonquin. The native hunters were skilled at stalking the wild animals in their homeland. The French wanted the furs and pelts of the animals they killed, particularly the rich, soft furs of the beaver. In Europe, hats made of beaver pelts were popular. The French in North America could make a good deal of money by trading with Indians for beaver furs and then selling the furs in Europe at a steep profit. This exchange became known as the fur trade.

The Huron and the Algonquin were eager participants in the fur trade. They wanted the goods the French offered. These included metal tools and guns, goods manufactured in Europe that the native people could not make themselves. To further win the favor of their native allies, the French helped them fight their traditional enemies, including the Iroquois.

Fighting with the British

French claims in North America did not go unchallenged. As France struggled to expand its settlements, British settlers and soldiers were arriving on the continent, some hoping to get in on the lucrative fur trade. In 1670, English king Charles II granted to the Hudson's Bay Company the right to trade on all lands drained by the waters of Hudson Bay. This organization began building trading posts and forts along the bay. The company eventually expanded westward, taking over swaths of land in what is now central and northern Canada. At its height, the Hudson's Bay Company was the largest landholder in the world.

As more British people arrived in Canada, tensions rose between the British and the French. The two groups, aided by their native allies, battled one another frequently. A turning point came in 1745, when the British took over the French fort at Louisbourg in Nova Scotia, which gave them control over Acadia. About ten years later, the British forced thousands of Acadians to leave their homes. Some returned to France, and others traveled to Quebec. Still others headed south to French-held lands in what is now the American state of Louisiana. Their descendants are called Cajuns.

To replace the French Acadians, the British sent shiploads of settlers from Scotland and Ireland to Acadia. The island of Nova Scotia—which means "New Scotland" in Latin—was given its name in honor of these early Scottish settlers.

British soldiers forced Acadians from their homes during the French and Indian War.

The British Take Charge

Between 1754 and 1763, the British and the French fought an all-out war for control of North America. The conflict is often called the French and Indian War, the name used by the British. In Canada, the decisive conflict was the 1759 Battle of the Plains of Abraham, which was fought near Quebec City. Marquis de Montcalm led the French force, while Major General James P. Wolfe commanded the British soldiers. Both Montcalm and Wolfe were killed in the battle, which ended with the defeat of the French. The British victory settled the long rivalry between the British and French in Canada. By the war's end, the British were firmly in charge.

The British, in red, quickly defeated the French at the Battle of the Plains of Abraham.

The British triumph came at a price. The war had been very expensive. The British government decided to pay for it by taxing the American colonists who lived to the south of Canada. The colonists resisted the taxes and even threatened to revolt to gain their independence from the British. The British feared that these threats might stir up trouble in Canada, where large numbers of French settlers were unhappy living under British rule. To encourage the loyalty of the French Canadians, the British government passed the Quebec Act of 1774. The law promised French Canadians that the British would not interfere with their way of life in several important ways. For instance, it guaranteed that the French of Quebec could keep their old legal system. It also allowed the French to practice their religion, Roman Catholicism. The Quebec Act was an important moment in the history of Canada. It ensured that the nation would embrace both the British and French customs of its settlers.

Creating Canada

The British strategy worked. Soon after the start of the American Revolution (1775–1783), the American army invaded Quebec. French Canadians there refused to join their cause, and the Americans were repelled by British troops.

Because Canada remained loyal to Great Britain, many Americans who supported the British government fled north during and after the war. In total, about forty thousand of these Loyalists moved to Canada. Most settled in present-day Nova Scotia, New Brunswick, and Ontario.

The opening of Canada's first Parliament in 1867 drew crowds.

During the late eighteenth and early nineteenth centuries, several British explorers, including Alexander Mackenzie and Simon Fraser, staged expeditions through what is now northwest Canada. Their explorations encouraged fur traders to come to the region. The traders soon began establishing settlements there.

Both in Canada and in Britain, many people felt a need to unite all the British-held lands in North America. Over many years, they worked to create a new government for Canada. The result was the British North America Act of 1867, also known as the Constitution Act. The act, passed by the British Parliament, established the Dominion of Canada. Canada retained ties to the British government, but beginning on July 1, 1867, it became an independent, largely self-governing nation.

At first the new nation was made up of just four provinces—Ontario, Quebec, New Brunswick, and Nova Scotia. Over the course of many years, the map of modern Canada took shape. During the 1870s, Manitoba, British Columbia, and Prince Edward Island became provinces. Saskatchewan and Alberta were added in 1905. Newfoundland (now called Newfoundland and Labrador) joined Canada in 1949. A large northern region, called the Northwest Territories,

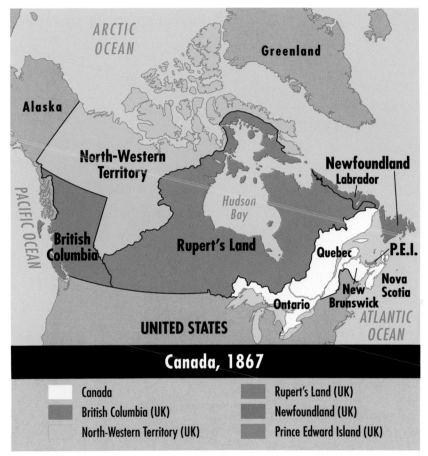

ARCTIC OCEAN

Greenland

Alaska

North-Western Territory

Newfoundland
Labrador

PACIFIC OCEAN

Hudson Bay

British Columbia

Rupert's Land

Quebec

P.E.I.

Nova Scotia

New Brunswick

Ontario

UNITED STATES

ATLANTIC OCEAN

Canada, 1867

	Canada		Rupert's Land (UK)
	British Columbia (UK)		Newfoundland (UK)
	North-Western Territory (UK)		Prince Edward Island (UK)

CAMP LOON

The Klondike Gold Rush

During Canada's early history, the Klondike was a nearly unpopulated area in the Northwest Territories. But in 1896, gold was discovered there. The discovery sparked a massive gold rush. Tens of thousands of people flooded into the area, hoping to get rich. The Klondike gold rush helped open this rugged region to settlement. Just two years after the rush began, Canada formally organized Yukon Territory, which includes the Klondike.

was divided to create two other territories—Yukon in 1898 and Nunavut in 1999.

A Growing Country

Although, after 1867, Canada was ruled by one national government, it was hardly a united country. The eastern provinces included a mix of British and French settlements that were largely isolated from one another. Native peoples, who felt no real allegiance to the Canadian government, inhabited much of Canada's western territory. The plains of Manitoba, Saskatchewan, and Alberta were home to many new immigrants from Europe. Most left their native countries to escape wars and poverty. They were largely drawn to the Canadian prairies because of the cheap and fertile farmland there.

Many people took the Canadian Pacific Railway to their new homes in the West. The trains had sleeping cars, with bunks that folded down so travelers could stretch out.

During the late nineteenth century, however, the east and west were gradually joined by railroads. By 1885, a transcontinental railroad stretched across the country, so now Canadians could easily travel all the way from the Atlantic to the Pacific.

While railroads helped unite Canada, they were a disaster for many of its people. The nonnatives the railroad brought west started taking over native lands. Some groups resisted

Métis Hero

In the late nineteenth century, activist Louis Riel fought for the rights of the Métis (people of mixed French and Indian ancestry) as their western homelands came under the control of the Canadian government. He led two resistance movements in which the Catholic Métis fought to protect their lands from being overrun by Protestant Canadians. During the Red River Rebellion (1869–1870), he negotiated with Parliament—Canada's lawmaking body—to establish the terms under which Manitoba would become a province of Canada. For his efforts, he is now celebrated as the "Father of Manitoba."

Riel fled Canada in fear of punishment for his involvement in the execution of a militiaman who tried to put down the Red River Rebellion. He lived in the United States for several years, before heading to present-day Saskatchewan to help the Métis there. Now convinced he was on a mission from God, Riel led the failed North-West Rebellion in 1885. Riel was found guilty of treason and executed. Today, many Canadians, especially Métis, view Riel as a folk hero who sacrificed his life to fight for his people.

these newcomers, but many eventually lost their land. Some were forced onto small territories, called reserves, by government officials.

Into the Twentieth Century

A test of Canadian unity came during World War I (1914–1918). Because of its British ties, Canada entered this European war on the side of Great Britain in 1914. At first, Canada asked only volunteers to fight, but soon a draft forced young Canadian men into military service. French Canadians, who felt little allegiance to Great Britain, were angered by the draft, and many resisted. In the end, the war proved a difficult

Native people and Canadian officials meet in 1881. In the 1880s, many native people were forced off their land.

In Flanders Fields

Among the thousands of Canadian soldiers who died during World War I was Lieutenant Colonel John McCrae. A graduate of the University of Toronto medical school, McCrae served as a medical officer in France. When he was not treating the injured, he wrote poetry. He is best known for his poem "In Flanders Fields." Told in the voice of the war dead buried in the region of Flanders, the first lines read, "In Flanders fields the poppies blow/Between the crosses, row on row."

"In Flanders Fields" is now known the world over. In Canada, musical versions of the poem are sung during ceremonies on Remembrance Day, a holiday that commemorates the end of World War I. On that day, people in Canada often wear red poppy pins in remembrance of the dead.

trial for all Canadians. More than sixty thousand Canadians died during the long and bloody conflict.

Canada suffered another blow in the 1930s. A worldwide economic depression left many Canadians without work, money, or hope. Adding to the misery, severe droughts in the western prairies led to poor harvests. Many farmers were unable to feed their families, much less make a living from their crops.

When World War II (1939–1945) began, Canada again sided with Britain. The war led to a significant change in Canadian life. In addition to sending soldiers overseas, Canada geared up its manufacturing industries to supply weapons and

French is an official language in Canada. In many parts of the country, signs are in both English and French.

machinery for its allies. After the war, manufacturing goods remained an important part of the Canadian economy. The rapid growth of these industries allowed Canada to prosper. The country's economy was further strengthened by the discovery of oil in Alberta in 1947.

People from other nations began flocking to Canada in the hope of finding jobs that paid well. Many of these people were from Asia and Africa. The high rate of immigration between 1941 and 1974 helped Canada double its population.

The Separatist Movement

While the rest of Canada was thriving, many people in Quebec felt they were being left behind. Life in this largely French-speaking province was still dominated by the Catholic Church, which resisted industrialization. Wanting the fruits of the nation's boom years like other Canadians, the French Canadians in Quebec, known as the Québécois, worked to reform their government to reduce the power of the church in the province. At the same time, the Québécois began to celebrate their French-influenced culture.

Some Québécois began to advocate separatism. They argued that the French Canadians of Quebec were so different from other Canadians that they would be better off if Quebec broke away from Canada and became an independent nation. The Canadian government resisted the separatist movement. To convince the Québécois that they could retain their culture and still be citizens of Canada, it instituted a number of reforms. The government began funding more French-speaking schools and appointing more French Canadians to important political posts. In 1969, it also adopted French as an official national language.

Despite these changes, some Québécois have continued to promote separatism. Three times—in 1980, 1995, and 2005—the people of Quebec voted on whether they wanted to secede, or separate, from Canada. Each time, the voters chose "no." In 1995, however, the vote was very close. About 50.5 percent voted against seceding, while 49.5 percent voted for it.

Even so, the government's efforts to improve conditions for French speakers have had a lasting impact. Since the early 1970s, Canadian policies have encouraged tolerance for all its citizens. These policies have not only benefited the French-speaking minority, but also native people and ethnic groups that have arrived in Canada more recently. Despite occasional conflicts, as a whole, Canadians take great pride in their ability to live peacefully with their neighbors, no matter their history or backgrounds.

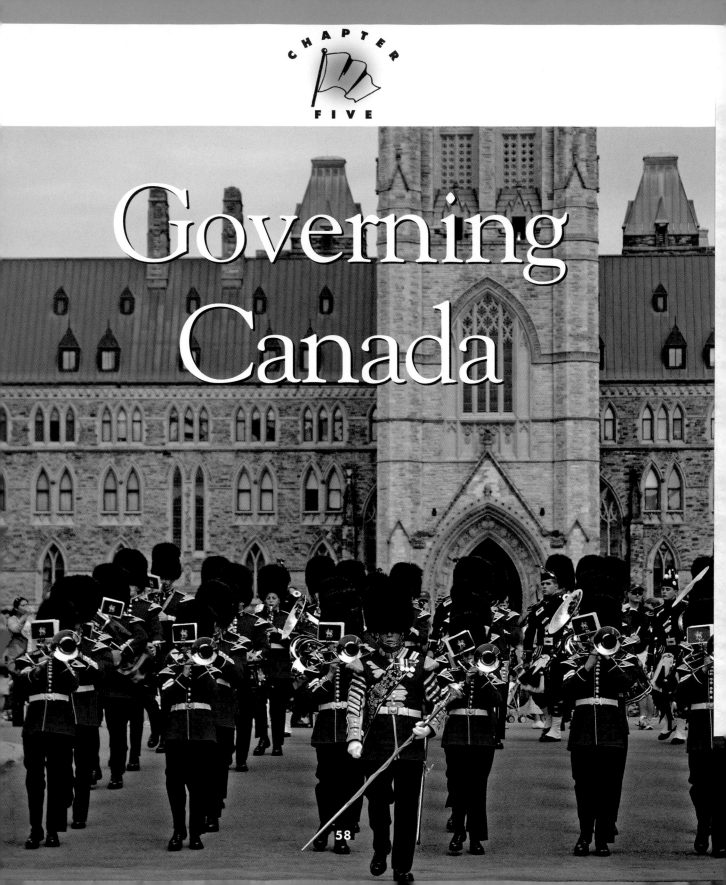

CHAPTER

FIVE

Governing
Canada

Opposite: **A band performs in honor of Canada Day, the day the country became independent.**

Canadians celebrate their country's independence day on July 1—the anniversary of the day in 1867 when Canada officially became a self-governing nation. Canada, however, still has some ties to the government of the United Kingdom (the modern country composed of England, Scotland, Wales, and Northern Ireland). For instance, Canada remains part of the Commonwealth of Nations, an association of independent nations made up of the United Kingdom and fifty-three other countries, including Australia, India, and South Africa. Great Britain once controlled almost all

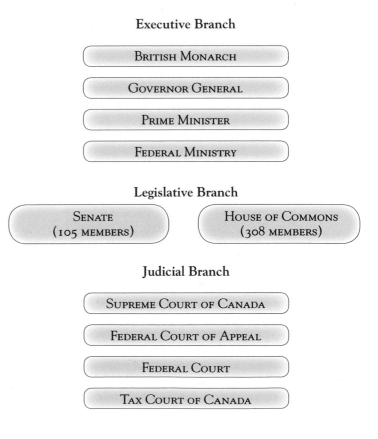

National Government of Canada

Executive Branch

- British Monarch
- Governor General
- Prime Minister
- Federal Ministry

Legislative Branch

- Senate (105 members)
- House of Commons (308 members)

Judicial Branch

- Supreme Court of Canada
- Federal Court of Appeal
- Federal Court
- Tax Court of Canada

A statue of Queen Victoria, who ruled the United Kingdom from 1837 to 1901, stands in front of the legislative building in Victoria, British Columbia.

the Commonwealth nations. About one-third of all people in the world live in a Commonwealth country.

The Executive Branch

Canada's old connections to Great Britain are seen in the structure of its federal, or national, government. The Canadian government is a constitutional monarchy. This means it is governed by a set of rules spelled out in a document called a constitution. At the same time, it recognizes the British monarch (king or queen) as Canada's head of state. Since the mid-twentieth century, Elizabeth II, the queen of Great Britain and head of the Commonwealth, has also been the queen of Canada.

Queen Elizabeth is part of the Canadian government's executive branch. This branch oversees the daily administration of the government. Even though she is formally Canada's head of state, the queen has little role in the day-to-day operation of the country. She is instead represented in the government by the governor general.

The queen appoints the governor general for a five-year term on the advice of the prime minister of Canada. The governor general is mostly a symbolic job. The prime minister is the person in the executive branch with the greatest real

Pierre Trudeau

Pierre Trudeau served as prime minister of Canada for more than fifteen years, during one of the most tumultuous periods in its history. Born in Montreal, Quebec, in 1919, he was of French and Scottish descent. After graduating with a law degree from the University of Montreal, Trudeau continued his studies in the United States, France, and England.

When Trudeau returned home, he founded a journal, *Cité Libre* (Free City), which called for reforms in Quebec's conservative government. He also began teaching law at the University of Montreal. He joined the Liberal Party and entered politics in 1965. Trudeau successfully won a seat in the House of Commons, and in 1968, battled more than a dozen rivals to become prime minister. He was the third French Canadian to hold that position.

Trudeau was an unusual choice. In a society that traditionally values people who speak softly and are humble, many saw him as arrogant and brash. But his charisma and energy made him popular with Canadians. They also generally supported his policies, which sought to use tax dollars to aid the nation's poorer provinces.

Trudeau met his greatest challenge as prime minister when activists from his native Quebec campaigned to create a separate nation. Trudeau strongly opposed the separatist movement. Largely because of his stance, voters chose to keep Canada intact.

Trudeau stepped down as prime minister in 1984. He died in 2000, shortly before turning eighty-one.

power. His or her role is similar to that of the president in the United States.

The prime minister is the leader of the political party with the most people in Parliament, Canada's lawmaking body. One of the prime minister's most important duties is to appoint the ministry. Ministry politicians head various departments of the Canadian government. For instance, there is a minister of health, of international trade, of national defense, and of the environment.

Making Laws

The Canadian Parliament is made up of two groups, or houses. The Senate has 105 members, who are appointed by the governor general in consultation with the prime minister. Once appointed, senators stay in their posts until they reach age seventy-five.

In practice, the Senate has limited power. It usually approves whatever laws are proposed by the lower house, known as the House of Commons. The House has 308 members, each representing a certain area, or district, within Canada. All Canadians age eighteen or older can vote for their house representative.

Canadians often vote for candidates based on their political party. Political parties are groups of citizens and politicians who share similar views about how a nation should be governed. The most important national parties in Canada today are the Conservative Party, the New Democratic Party, and the Liberal Party. Other important national parties are the

Green Party and the Bloc Québécois. The Green Party is particularly interested in environmental issues. The Bloc Québécois calls for the separation of Quebec from Canada.

National elections in Canada are held at least once every five years. A government is elected for a four-year period, but that can be legally extended an additional year. The prime minister, however, can choose to hold an election early. The House of Commons can also force an election by calling for a vote of no confidence in the present government.

Prime Minister Stephen Harper was returned to office when his Conservative Party won a major victory in national elections in 2011.

National Anthem

"O Canada" was named Canada's national anthem on July 1, 1980, one hundred years after it was written. Calixa Lavallée wrote the music, and Adolphe-Basile Routhier wrote the original French lyrics. These lyrics were translated into English in 1906. Robert Stanley Weir wrote different English lyrics in 1908. The English lyrics have since been revised twiced.

English lyrics

O Canada!
Our home and native land!
True patriot love in all thy sons command.
With glowing hearts we see thee rise,
The True North strong and free!
From far and wide,
O Canada, we stand on guard for thee.
God keep our land glorious and free!
O Canada, we stand on guard for thee.
O Canada, we stand on guard for thee.

French lyrics

Ô Canada!
Terre de nos aïeux,
Ton front est ceint de fleurons glorieux!
Car ton bras sait porter l'épée,
Il sait porter la croix!
Ton histoire est une épopée
Des plus brillants exploits.
Et ta valeur, de foi trempée,
Protégera nos foyers et nos droits.
Protégera nos foyers et nos droits.

The Courts of Canada

The judicial branch of Canada's national government consists of a court system that interprets and enforces Canada's laws. Its most powerful body is the Supreme Court of Canada. The nine judges on this court are chosen by the prime minister and formally appointed by the governor general. The Supreme Court considers cases from lower courts to determine if their rulings go against Canada's constitution.

The lower courts in the nation's court system include the Federal Court, the Tax Court of Canada, and the Federal Court of Appeal. The Federal Court hears cases in specific areas, such as immigration disputes and legal matters dealing

The Capital City

Ottawa, Canada's capital city, is a blend of old and new. Situated on the Ottawa River, it was a small backwater settlement until the mid-nineteenth century, when Queen Victoria of England selected it to be Canada's capital. It is now home to an ethnically diverse population of approximately eight hundred thousand. Although its main business is government, in recent years the growing high-tech industry has fueled its economy. As a result, gleaming new office buildings intermix with centuries-old architecture. Ottawa's most impressive landmark is Parliament, where Canada's lawmakers meet. It also has many museums, including the National Gallery of Canada, the Bytown Museum, and the Canadian Museum of Civilization. Parks and gardens dot the city. During the summer, visitors can tour Ottawa in boats traveling the Rideau Canal, which cuts through the middle of the city. In the winter, the canal freezes, creating the world's largest ice rink.

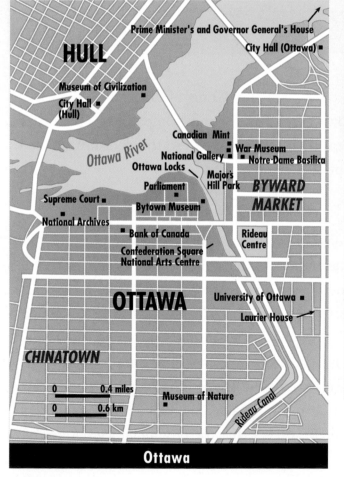

The Supreme Court Building is in Ottawa. Court hearings are open to the public.

with native peoples. The Tax Court of Canada resolves issues about taxes owed by citizens and companies. The Federal Court of Appeal rules on challenges to the decisions made by judges in the other federal courts.

Provincial Governments

The governments of provinces have three branches that mirror those of the national government. The executive branch of each province has a lieutenant governor, appointed by the British monarch, who serves a role similar to that of the governor general. The real leader in each province, however, is the premier. Like the prime minister on the national level, the premier is the head of the most powerful party in the province.

Each province has a lawmaking body that resembles the national Parliament, except that the provincial legislatures have only one house instead of two. In most provinces, the legislatures are called assemblies. In Nova Scotia and Newfoundland and Labrador, the legislature is known as the House of Assembly. In Quebec, it is called the National Assembly.

Major national parties generally field candidates in provincial elections. But voters often choose candidates from one or two local parties that are concerned with issues of particular importance to the people of the province. Some voters choose candidates from the same political party in national and provincial elections. But others change parties when choosing provincial representatives.

Like the national government, provincial governments have a judicial branch. Provincial courts include the Court of Appeal, the Court of Queen's Bench, the Superior Court, the Supreme Court, and the Court of Justice. The national and provincial judicial systems are all based on British law with

The Maple Leaf Flag

In 1964, Canadian prime minister Lester B. Pearson announced that he wanted the nation to adopt a new and distinctive flag. The flag was to be used in the upcoming celebrations of the one hundredth anniversary of Canada's founding. The Senate and House of Commons formed a committee to consider possible designs. The one they chose has a white square in the center with a red rectangle to the left and right. In the middle of the white square is an eleven-pointed red maple leaf. This flag was formally adopted on February 15, 1965. Speaker of the Senate Maurice Bourget stated, "The flag is the symbol of the nation's unity, for it, beyond any doubt, represents all the citizens of Canada without distinction of race, language, belief, or opinion."

one exception. The province of Quebec relies on the French civil code, a French system of laws. Canada is unique in using two distinct legal systems.

Federal and Provincial Duties

In general, the federal and provincial governments deal with different, yet overlapping, concerns. The federal government is responsible for national defense, trade, international relations, and native affairs, among many other things. The provincial governments' responsibilities include education, health care, law enforcement, and road building.

The British monarch has representatives at both the federal and provincial levels of Canadian government. Edward Roberts was lieutenant governor of Newfoundland and Labrador, and Michaëlle Jean was governor general of Canada.

Canada's constitution generally made the national government far stronger than provincial governments, much to the dismay of provincial politicians. Throughout much of Canadian history, the provincial governments have sought additional powers. In recent times, representatives of both levels of government have come together several times to try to rework the balance of power. Fighting among the provinces defeated these efforts.

Territorial and Municipal Governments

The three territories in Canada—Yukon, Nunavut, and the Northwest Territories—have a different relationship with the federal government. Provinces and their governments have certain powers granted to them by the Canadian constitution. Territories, on the other hand, are much more dependent on the authority of the federal government.

A commissioner heads each territorial government. The commissioner acts as the national government's representative in the territory. Territories also have government leaders, whose role is similar to that of premiers in the provinces. In addition, they have legislative assemblies, to which in recent years the federal government has given increasing responsibility.

Municipal governments are local governments that provide services to the people of a particular city, town, or county. Municipal services often include garbage collection, public transit, and animal control. The routine duties of local governments might not be glamorous, but they play a central role in making Canadian communities comfortable places to live.

In the Money

CANADIANS HAVE LONG EARNED THEIR LIVELIHOODS by making good use of their country's rich and fertile lands. Centuries ago, native nations thrived through hunting and fishing. Soon after the first Europeans arrived, the trade in beaver furs attracted many people to Canada. Other immigrants came to make a living by turning its forests into timber and clearing its western grasslands to create productive farms and ranches.

Making use of Canada's vast natural resources is still profitable. But since the middle of the twentieth century, the country's economy has been transformed. Many new industries—from manufacturing to banking to high tech—have found a home in Canada, helping make it one of the wealthiest nations on the globe.

Farms, Forests, and Fish

Older industries, such as farming and fishing, have long been important to Canada. But new technologies have made these industries more productive than ever. For instance, farm

Opposite: **Lumber is one of Canada's most valuable exports.**

Grains grow well on the Canadian plains. Canada is one of the world's top barley producers.

machinery allows Canada to grow more than enough food for its entire population, although only about 2 percent of its workforce is employed in agriculture. Most of Canada's farms are found on the western plains and prairies. The region's leading crops include barley, canola, oats, and rye, but the most important crop is wheat. Canada is the second-largest wheat exporter in the world. Grains grown on the plains are also used as feed for livestock, most notably cows and hogs. Other important crops include tobacco, grown in Ontario, and potatoes, grown on Prince Edward Island.

Half of Canada's land is covered with forests. The forests are largely owned by provinces, which lease the lands to lumber companies. In the north, more than three hundred towns have been established just for workers in the lumber industry. In addition to lumber, Canada's forests produce wood pulp and paper, which are exported to countries around the world.

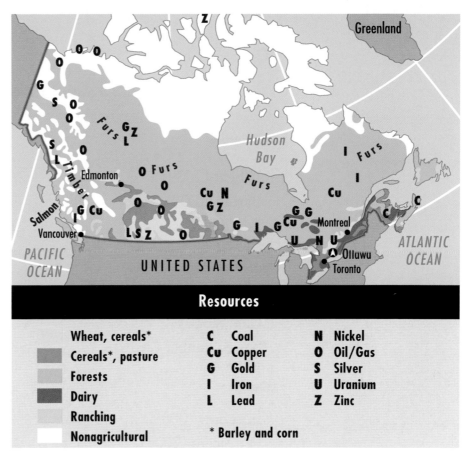

Resources

	Wheat, cereals*	**C**	Coal	**N**	Nickel
	Cereals*, pasture	**Cu**	Copper	**O**	Oil/Gas
	Forests	**G**	Gold	**S**	Silver
	Dairy	**I**	Iron	**U**	Uranium
	Ranching	**L**	Lead	**Z**	Zinc
	Nonagricultural				

* Barley and corn

Its coastal waters ensure that Canada remains a leading producer of fish and seafood. The Pacific coast is known for its salmon and clams, while the waters of the Atlantic yield lobsters, crabs, shrimps, and scallops. Today, seafood not consumed in Canada is often frozen or canned for sale to other countries. In recent years, the Canadian government has become increasingly aware of the dangers that overfishing poses to the fish population. It has been working to find ways to make sure the fish populations stay healthy. It wants to protect this valuable natural resource.

What Canada Grows, Makes, and Mines

Agriculture

Wheat (2009)	26,514,600 metric tons
Barley (2009)	9,517,200 metric tons
Beef (2008)	1,288,070 metric tons

Manufacturing

Food products (2010)	$82,147,100,000 in sales
Cars (2010)	2,071,016 units
Sawed lumber (2010)	1,882,663,721 metric feet

Mining

Iron ore (2006)	33,551,000 metric tons
Petroleum (2007)	25,345,000 metric tons
Aluminum (2007)	3,083,000 metric tons

Mining and Energy

Even more important to the economy is mining. Canada's rich mineral deposits, especially in the Canadian Shield region, make the country a leading producer of iron ore, aluminum, nickel, copper, zinc, lead, silver, titanium, and uranium. Canada also has more than thirty active gold mines, mostly in Ontario and Quebec. Diamonds are mined in the Northwest Territories. Canada's lands also yield materials, such as sand, gravel, and stone, used in manufacturing and construction.

Big Nickel

Sudbury, in northern Ontario, is home to one of Canada's oddest attractions—Big Nickel. Standing 30 feet (9 m) high, this massive sculpture depicts a 1951 Canadian nickel. Big Nickel was the brainchild of a Sudbury fireman named Ted Szilva. The city was looking for a way to celebrate the one hundredth anniversary of its founding. Szilva proposed the idea for Big Nickel, which would highlight the city's history as a center for mining nickel. When city officials did not seem interested, Szilva worked to finance Big Nickel privately. His efforts paid off when Big Nickel was unveiled in 1964. Over time, the park around Big Nickel expanded to include more attractions, including a carousel, a train, and a model of an underground mine. Its grounds are also home to Science North, a science museum housed in two buildings in the shape of snowflakes.

Canada also plays an important role worldwide in the production of energy. Coal mining in western Canada has long provided an energy source used to create electricity and manufacture steel. More recently, Canada has been tapping into vast deposits of oil and natural gas in Alberta and Saskatchewan. Oil reserves in the Athabasca tar sands in northeastern Alberta are particularly extensive. The sands contain the largest known reserves of oil in the world. Geologists believe the area has twice as much oil as Saudi Arabia, now the world's largest oil exporter. Removing the oil from the sands is very difficult, however, so it is expensive.

Money Facts

In Canada, there are no $1 bills. Instead, Canadians use $1 and $2 coins, which are known as the loonie and the toonie. The loonie got its name because it features an image of a common loon, Canada's national bird. The toonie features an image of a polar bear. Its nickname is just a short way of saying "two loonies." Canada also mints coins valued at 1¢, 5¢, 10¢, 25¢, and 50¢.

Canada produces bills worth $5, $10, $20, $50, and $100. All have a portrait of a prime minister on the front, except for the $20 bill, which features Queen Elizabeth II. On the other side are images that celebrate different aspects of Canadian life. For example, the

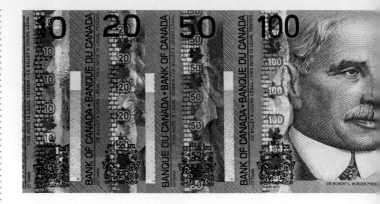

theme of the $20 bill is arts and culture. It shows pictures of four works by Bill Reid, a First Nations artist who spent most of his life in British Columbia. In 2011, 1.00 Canadian dollar equaled 1.03 U.S. dollar.

Many of Canada's rivers are used to produce hydroelectric power. Hydroelectric plants harness the power of water to make electricity. Canada has two of the largest hydroelectric power plants in the world. One is found on the Churchill River in Newfoundland and Labrador, and the other is located on the La Grande River in Quebec. Waterways throughout Canada have smaller hydroelectric plants. Except on the dry plains, these plants provide all the electrical power Canadians need.

Manufacturing in Canada

With plenty of natural resources and energy sources, Canada in recent years has become a manufacturing powerhouse. More than 450,000 Canadians now work in factories and other businesses that manufacture goods for sale. Manufactured items

made in Canada include transportation equipment, industrial machinery, chemicals, plastics, wood and paper, food products, and electrical equipment.

The majority of Canada's manufacturing plants are in Ontario and Quebec. Ontario is the center of automaking in Canada. Quebec, especially Montreal, is known for its clothing and textile industries.

The growth of manufacturing has also fueled the construction industry. Since the mid-twentieth century, more and

Bombardier Aerospace is the world's third-largest producer of nonmilitary jets. It is based in Quebec.

The Confederation Bridge stretches 8 miles (13 km) across the Northumberland Strait that separates New Brunswick and Prince Edward Island.

more Canadians have moved to cities to find jobs. This has increased the need for new housing, manufacturing plants, and office buildings. Many roads, bridges, and railways also had to be built to transport workers and goods.

Canada now boasts one of the greatest transportation systems in the world. Its vast train system covers more than 50,000 miles (80,000 km). Its three hundred commercial ports welcome some one hundred thousand ships each year.

Free Trade

In 1994, Canada negotiated a historic agreement with the United States and Mexico. The North American Free Trade Agreement, also known as NAFTA, made it cheaper and easier for the three nations to trade goods with one another. Taxes would no longer be collected on goods traded between the countries. As a result of NAFTA, about 75 percent of Canada's international export trade is with the United States. Canadian exports to the United States include oil, wood products, and metals, while it imports American industrial equipment, plastics, and computers.

Canada's many bridges include the enormous Confederation Bridge, which opened in 1997. Connecting Prince Edward Island to the New Brunswick mainland, this engineering wonder is the longest marine bridge ever built. Perhaps most impressive of all is the Trans-Canada Highway. Stretching from St. John's in Newfoundland to Victoria in British Columbia, this highway, the world's longest national road, is 4,860 miles (7,821 km) long.

Service Industries

Despite manufacturing's importance to the Canadian economy, it employs only about 13 percent of the Canadian people. About six times more Canadians now have jobs in service industries. They work in fields such as finance, real estate, transportation, insurance, and communication. The government employs many service workers, including teachers, doctors, and garbage collectors.

Other service workers are employed in stores. Canada's largest center for retail trade is the West Edmonton Mall in Alberta. This huge shopping complex covers forty-eight city blocks. In addition to eight hundred shops, one hundred restaurants, and two hotels, it houses the world's largest indoor amusement park and tallest indoor bungee tower.

Another growing service industry is tourism. With its beautiful landscapes and sophisticated cities, Canada attracts visitors from around the world. Toronto, Montreal, and Vancouver offer tourists a host of cultural attractions, from museums to historical sites, as well as great dining and shop-

A waiter prepares to serve food. Most Canadians work in service industries.

Canoeists head across Moraine Lake in Banff National Park. About four million people visit Banff each year.

ping opportunities. But Canada is especially popular with people looking for outdoor adventures. The country is full of parks and sporting facilities. Tourists can ski in Alberta, golf in Saskatchewan, hunt in Manitoba, and watch for whales in British Columbia. The territory of Nunavut provides some of the most exotic experiences for visitors to Canada. In this Arctic region, tourists can enjoy kayaking; look for whales, seals, and polar bears; or even go iceberg watching. In the summer months, the breaking ice along the shoreline creates a dramatic and unforgettable sight.

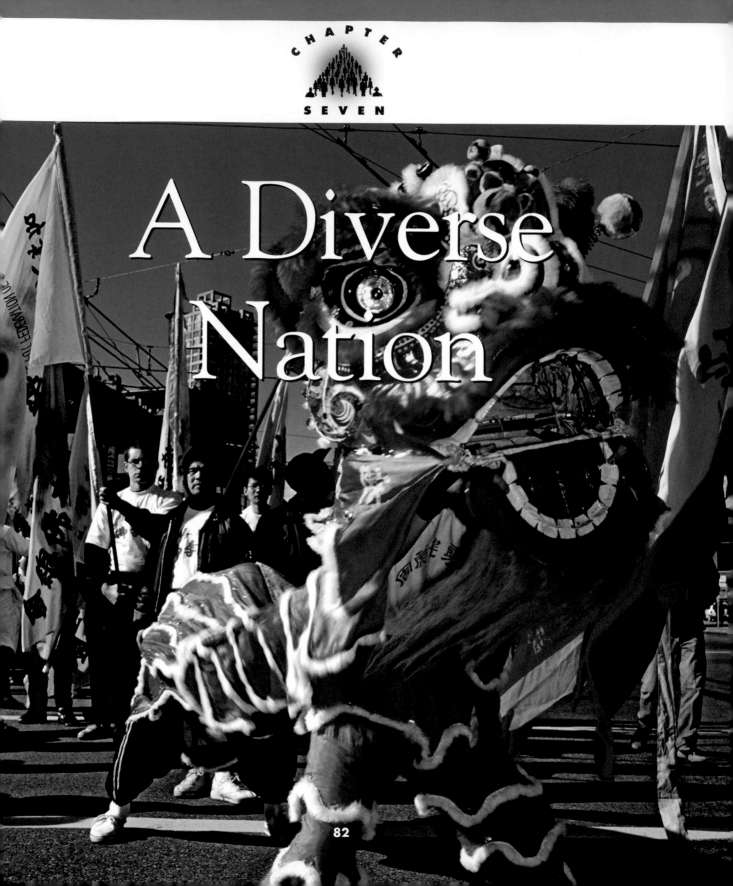

A Diverse Nation

FROM ITS VERY BEGINNINGS, CANADA HAS BEEN A LAND OF many peoples. In the past and in the present, these groups have sometimes come into conflict. But both the people and the government of today's Canada are committed to creating a multicultural society. Their goal is to ensure that all people, no matter their cultural background, are treated with respect.

Opposite: **Dragon dancers are part of the parade at Chinese New Year in Vancouver, British Columbia. Many cities in Canada have large Chinese populations.**

French Canadians

In the eighteenth century, the British beat the French in the battle for control of what is now Canada. Today, almost three out of every ten Canadians is of British ancestry. But French ancestry is still common, and French Canadians are the second-largest ethnic group in the country. Many French settlers resisted adopting the culture of the British settlers. They fought to keep their own way of life, which included practicing the Catholic religion and speaking the French language.

Most French Canadians now fall into one of two groups. The Acadians are the descendants of French speakers from the Maritime Provinces (New Brunswick, Nova Scotia, and

Population of Major Canadian Cities (2006)

City	Population
Toronto	2,503,281
Montreal	1,620,693
Calgary	988,193
Ottawa	812,129
Edmonton	730,372

Prince Edward Island). The province of New Brunswick has a particularly large number of Acadians. In recent years, Acadians have fought for their children to be able to attend schools where classes are taught in French.

The larger group of French Canadians lives in Quebec. Called the Québécois, they have fought since the 1960s to have more influence in the Canadian government. They also have sought to improve job prospects for French speakers. Some Québécois activists believe that, because of their cultural roots, French Canadians are fundamentally different from their fellow countrymen. The Québécois are the driving force behind the separatist movement, which wants to see Quebec break away from Canada and become a separate country.

A Bilingual Nation

Many French speakers in Quebec campaigned for Canada to adopt French as an official language. The Canadian Parliament responded in 1969 by passing the Official Languages Act. It stated that Canada was to be bilingual. It would have two official languages—English and French. The government of the province of New Brunswick also decided to become bilingual. Since 1982, however, all provinces have been required to provide children the choice of attending an English-language or a French-language school.

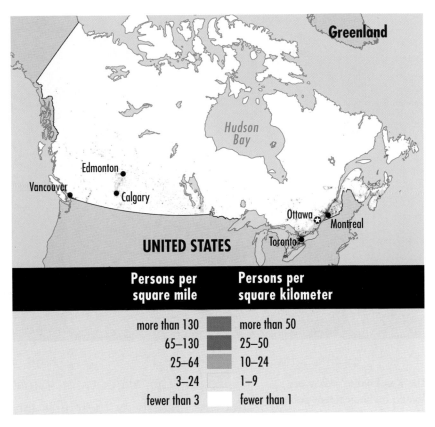

Persons per square mile	Persons per square kilometer
more than 130	more than 50
65–130	25–50
25–64	10–24
3–24	1–9
fewer than 3	fewer than 1

Even though Canada is bilingual, most of its people are not. The act meant that all federal government services had to be provided in both languages. No individual Canadian is required to learn a second language, although about 15 percent of Canadians are fluent in both French and English. Especially in Ontario and Quebec, being bilingual is very useful for professionals and businesspeople.

The Kwakwaka'wakw are famed for their totem poles. The world's tallest totem poles top 100 feet (30 m).

Today, the majority of Canadians—about 59 percent— identify English as their first language. About 21.5 percent consider themselves primarily French speakers, while another 19.5 have a different first language.

Native Peoples

Many of Canada's native peoples still speak their traditional language. Throughout Canada, a total of about sixty native languages are still in use. They include Cree, Inuktitut, and Ojibwe.

Many native Canadians belong to First Nations groups. The Canadian government recognizes more than six hundred First Nations bands. First Nations include the Dene, Iroquois, Cree, Nootka, Huron, and Kwakwaka'wakw (also called the Kwakiutl).

Other native Canadians are Inuits. Their ancestors arrived in the region during a later migration than those of the First Nations peoples. (The Inuits used to be called Eskimos, but in Canada that term is now considered offensive.) Many Inuits live in Yukon, Nunavut, and the Northwest Territories. Together, First Nations peoples and Inuits now make up about 2 percent of all Canadian people.

The Métis are another Canadian group with native ancestry. Long ago, the term applied to people of mixed First Nations and French heritage. More often today, it refers to people whose ancestry is a blend of any First Nations and European group. The Métis have long suffered from poverty and discrimination. Various organizations, particularly the Métis National Council, are seeking to improve the lives of the Métis and increase their voice in Canada's government.

An Inuit woman wears a modern version of a traditional parka, which is designed with room to carry a baby and has a hood that can cover both mother and child.

Nunavut

Canada's map saw an important change in 1999. That year, the eastern half of the Northwest Territories became a new territory called Nunavut. The territory is home to about thirty thousand people, mostly Inuits. Nunavut has four official languages: Inuktitut and Inuinnaqtun (two languages traditionally spoken by the Inuit), English, and French. The word *Nunavut* means "our land" in Inuktitut.

A Nation of Immigrants

Many Canadians trace their ancestry from countries other than France and Great Britain. They are either recent immigrants or the descendants of earlier immigrants. Canada's first wave of immigration began in the late nineteenth century. Many who came were attracted by the opportunity to purchase cheap land in the western provinces, which by then were easily accessible by train. Most of these immigrants came from Europe. They included Germans, Italians, Scandinavians, Dutch, and Poles.

More recently, immigrants from Asian and African nations have arrived in large numbers. Many are from China, India, the Philippines, and Middle Eastern countries. Toronto, Ontario, is the most popular destination for immigrants, although many Chinese immigrants choose to live in Vancouver, British Columbia. Vancouver now has the largest number of people of Chinese ancestry—381,500—of any city outside of Asia.

Because of immigration, Canada is home to more than two

Girls jump rope in Fort McMurray, Alberta. Canadians trace their roots to nations all over the world.

hundred different ethnic groups. Although most immigrants learn to speak English or French, many continue to speak their own native languages. Because of recent immigration trends, Chinese is now the third most common language in Canada. Other languages commonly heard in Canada include German, Italian, Spanish, and Punjabi (a language spoken in a region of India and Pakistan).

Canadian Ethnic Groups	
British ancestry	28%
French ancestry	23%
Other European ancestry	15%
Mixed ancestry	26%
Other (primarily Asian, African, and Arab) ancestry	6%
First Nations (American Indian, Inuit, and Métis) ancestry	2%

Both the United States and Canada are largely nations of immigrants, but the two countries have traditionally taken a different approach to immigration. Americans tend to want new immigrant groups to adopt the culture of the majority. The United States is often called a "melting pot." Everyone's culture melts together to create the American way of life.

Canadians, in contrast, are less insistent that new immigrants give up their old ways. They instead see their country as a "cultural mosaic." A mosaic is a pattern or a picture made from different colored tiles. Each tile remains intact even as, taken together, they create a bigger picture. Similarly, ethnic groups in Canada retain their own ways while their culture contributes to the bigger picture of what it means to be Canadian.

Children of different cultural backgrounds have their faces painted at a street fair in Montreal.

Indian Canadians celebrate a victory by Canada's hockey team during the 2010 Olympics.

To help promote this idea, the Canadian Parliament passed the Official Multiculturalism Act in 1988. This law provides equal rights to all Canadians, no matter their cultural background, race, or religion. Since its passage, the government has started numerous programs to help immigrants adjust to their new homeland and find jobs. It has also organized campaigns designed to stop racism and make all Canadians more accepting of people different from themselves. In schools, the government also promotes lessons that explain the history of various groups in Canada and celebrate their contributions to Canadian society.

Despite the many differences among themselves, Canadians generally have embraced multiculturalism. Most are proud that, around the world, Canada is viewed as an especially tolerant nation. It is just that tolerance that continues to attract new immigrants looking for a better life.

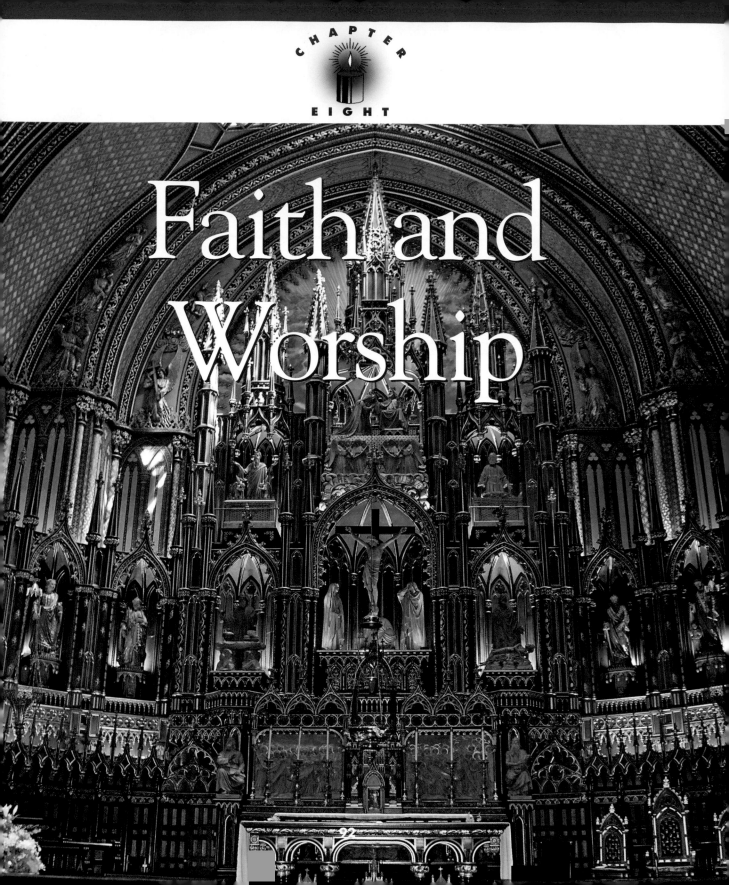

Faith and Worship

From Canada's earliest days, the majority of its citizens have been Christians. In the 2006 census, seven out of ten Canadians said that they were members of a Christian religion. Yet, it would be wrong to call modern Canada a Christian nation. Canada has no official state religion, and the government encourages tolerance of all religions among its people.

Roman Catholicism

Roman Catholicism is the most common religion in Canada. About 43 percent of all Canadians are Catholic. Catholicism has a long history in Canada. In 1543, members of the Cartier expedition celebrated the first Catholic mass in Canada on the Gaspé Peninsula. Catholicism was also the religion of other early French explorers, traders, and settlers in Canada.

Among the first colonists of New France were Catholic priests. They came to Canada on a mission. The priests wanted to convert the native people to Christianity. Generally, the people of New France had little respect for the native people's

Religions of Canadians	
Roman Catholic	43.2%
No religion	16.2%
United Church	9.6%
Anglican	6.9%
Baptist	2.5%
Lutheran	2.0%
Muslim	2.0%
Presbyterian	1.4%
Pentecostal	1.2%
Jewish	1.1%
Buddhist	1.0%
Hindu	1.0%
Other	11.9%

Roman Catholic worshippers gather in St. Joseph's Oratory of Mount Royal in Montreal. More than 40 percent of Canadians are Roman Catholic.

own religions. The priests insisted that native converts abandon their old religion completely. Some natives willingly converted to Catholicism, but others resisted the priests and maintained their traditional beliefs.

Catholicism remains an important social force in much of Canada, particularly in New Brunswick and Quebec, where about three-fifths of Canadian Catholics live. Although weekly church attendance has decreased throughout Canada in recent years, Catholicism still plays a significant role in the lives of many French Canadians. In several provinces, including Ontario, students can attend Catholic schools funded by the Canadian government.

Protestantism was first introduced to Canada by the British settlers and traders who took control of New France in the eighteenth century. Like Catholics, Protestants are Christians. But unlike Catholics, they belong to a wide variety of smaller sects, each of which has slightly different beliefs.

The most common Protestant religion in Canada is the United Church of Canada. The church was formed in 1925 by Canadian followers of several faiths, including Presbyterians, Methodists, and Congregationalists. Church services in the United Church tend to be informal. Each congregation is permitted to choose its own clergy and worship in whatever style it sees fit. The United Church is also liberal on a number of

Lutherans attend a service in Edmonton, Alberta.

social issues. Today, almost three million Canadians belong to some 3,500 United Church congregations.

The nation's third-largest religion is the Anglican Church of Canada. Formerly known as the Church of England in Canada, it was introduced to Canada by British settlers more than four hundred years ago. Now, about two million Canadians are Anglicans. Almost half of them live in Ontario.

Other Protestant groups have fairly small numbers of Canadian followers. Baptists and Lutherans are both largely concentrated in the Maritime Provinces.

The Doukhobors

In the seventeenth century, a group of Russians broke away from the Russian Orthodox Church. They challenged religious authorities by claiming that God did not exist in church, but within each human being. For many years, they were persecuted for their beliefs. They were mocked as Doukhobors, or Spirit-Wrestlers, a name they came to embrace.

In 1899, Russia allowed 7,500 Doukhobors to leave the country for Saskatchewan, Canada. Most eventually moved to British Columbia. There, they established communal settlements, where they shared their land and wealth. After repeated clashes with provincial officials and with each other, the Doukhobors lost much of their land holdings. But about 25,000 descendants of the original Doukhobors still live in Canada. About one-third of them observe their old traditions, including speaking the Russian language and practicing their ancestors' religion.

Non-Christian Groups

About 10 percent of Canadians belong to non-Christian faiths. Many live in large cities, such as Toronto, Montreal, and Vancouver.

Jewish people have the longest history in Canada of any non-Christian group. They first came to Canada from western Europe during the eighteenth century and settled in Montreal, where in 1768 they established Canada's first synagogue (a Jewish house of worship). Jewish Canadians soon began living in other cities as well, particularly Toronto. Because of Jewish immigration to Canada, especially after World War II, the country now has the fifth-largest Jewish population in the world. In 2006, about 350,000 Canadians identified themselves as Jewish.

A Jewish synagogue in Toronto. Toronto has the largest Jewish community in Canada.

Muslims in Montreal observe the end of Ramadan, the holiest month in the Muslim calendar.

In recent years, many immigrants to Canadian urban centers have come from Asia and Africa. They have introduced several new religions into Canadian society. The most common is Islam, which is now the fastest growing religion in Canada. Islam is practiced by about 1.6 billion people throughout the world. Like Christianity and Judaism, it recognizes one god.

Muslims—people who practice Islam—have long been present in Canada. The country's first census, taken in 1871, recorded a total of thirteen Muslims then living there.

Muslims have become a significant minority in the last few decades. More than six hundred thousand Canadians—about 2 percent of the total population—are Muslims.

Sikhism was introduced to Canada by about 5,000 laborers from the Punjab region of India who came to British Columbia in the late nineteenth century. About half of the country's Sikh population, which numbers about 278,000, still lives in this province. Other Asian religions practiced in Canada include Hinduism, Buddhism, and the Baha'i faith.

Girls in Toronto attend the Vaisakhi parade, which celebrates Sikh culture.

The Kirpan Controversy

The *kirpan* is a ceremonial sword that Sikhs are supposed to wear at all times. In Canada, the kirpan has inspired several important court cases dealing with freedom of religion. A Quebec court found that students did not have a right to wear a kirpan because it violated bans against weapons in schools. In 2006, however, the Supreme Court of Canada overruled this decision. It maintains that such bans interfere with the religious rights of Sikhs.

About 16 percent of Canadians say they do not belong to any organized religion. Many nonreligious Canadians live along the nation's west coast, particularly in the city of Vancouver. Some are atheists, people who do not believe in God. Others are agnostics, who say they do not know whether or not God exists. Several organizations have been established to express the views of nonbelievers. Humanist Canada, for instance, is a nonprofit group that works to keep religion separate from government policies in Canada.

Native Religions

Long before the arrival of Europeans in their lands, the natives of Canada had their own religions. These religions varied greatly from group to group. But in general, native peoples used their ceremonies and their religious stories to understand the natural world and the creatures in it. For many groups, religious leaders were also healers who helped care for the ill.

The ceremonies of native peoples of British Columbia, such as the Kwakwaka'wakw, were particularly elaborate. Throughout the rainy winter, they performed these rites, with dancers often wearing enormous painted wooden masks.

As Canadian natives lost control of their lands, the Canadian government encouraged them to abandon their traditional ways, including their religious beliefs. It even outlawed a ceremony called the potlatch, which was important to groups on the west coast. During the potlatch, a host lavished his guests with gifts and food.

Despite these measures, native religions survived. Now, Canada's native peoples are free to worship as they wish. While many are Christian, others retain their traditional beliefs. Like their ancestors, they gather for ceremonies to celebrate the natural world.

Kwakwaka'wakw people honor the dead as part of a potlatch ceremony.

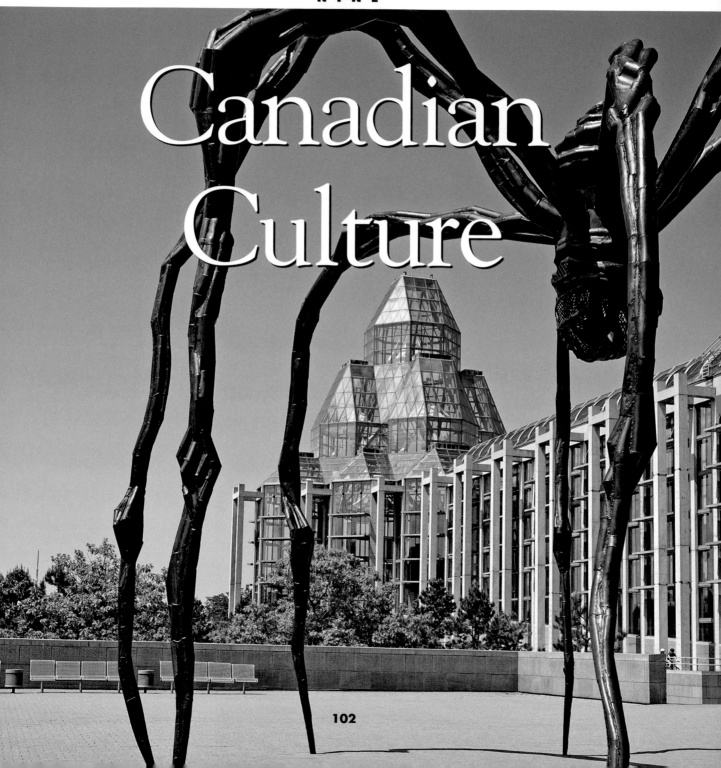

Canadian Culture

IN 1920, SEVEN CANADIAN PAINTERS—FRANKLIN CARMICHAEL, Lawren Harris, A. Y. Jackson, Frank Johnston, Arthur Lismer, J. E. H. MacDonald, and Frederick Varley—held an exhibition in an art gallery in Toronto, Ontario. Their works were landscapes, colorful expressions of the Canadian wilderness. In many ways, their paintings looked like those of European artists. But, at the same time, they showed something new. These Canadian painters, who became known as the Group of Seven, were using their talent to create art about Canada from a Canadian perspective.

At first, Canadians were confused by the Group of Seven. The idea of a uniquely Canadian artist seemed odd to them. Both critics and the public disliked the Toronto exhibition. Soon, however, the art show traveled to London, England, where it received rave reviews. This reception made Canadians, especially Canadian artists, reevaluate what the Group of Seven was doing. They became excited by the idea that they did not have to imitate European art. They could create their own style of painting, sculpture, music, theater, and literature that represented their lives as Canadians.

Opposite: **A giant spider sculpture stands in front of the National Gallery in Ottawa.**

Justin Bieber is one of the world's most popular singers. He was raised in Stratford, Ontario.

Ever since then, Canadian artists have worked to find their own voice. They are encouraged by the Canada Council, which the Canadian government established in 1957. This organization helps Canadian artists by providing them with grants and other support.

Making Music

One of the areas in which Canadian artists have made their greatest mark is music. Many Canadian singers are known around the world. Neil Young, Joni Mitchell, Leonard Cohen, and Alanis Morissette are famous for singing personal songs they wrote themselves. Shania Twain and k.d. lang are country and pop music stars, while Justin Bieber is a sensation in the world of pop.

In addition to these English-language singers, Canada has also produced many artists who sing in French. The most famous is Quebec-born Celine Dion. To broaden her audience, Dion learned English and has since scored many international hits, including the best-selling "My Heart Will Go On."

Canada has also made noteworthy contributions to the world of jazz music. Several jazz greats, such as pianist Oscar Peterson and trumpeter Maynard Ferguson, hailed from Canada. Montreal also hosts the most famous jazz festival in the world. Every July, jazz lovers crowd the city to attend some 650 showcases for more than three thousand musical artists.

Singing Superstar

Singing in both French and English, Montreal native Celine Dion has become an international superstar. The youngest of fourteen children, Dion began her singing career performing for patrons of her parents' restaurant. At a young age, she was discovered by René Angélil, who would become her manager and later her husband. While still in her teens, she started recording in French and appearing at music festivals around the world.

Known for her stirring ballads and spirited dance tracks, Dion sells out concerts around the globe. She remains especially identified with the song "My Heart Will Go On" from the movie *Titanic*. The record won an Academy Award for Best Song and became one of the biggest selling singles of all time.

The Royal Winnipeg Ballet is Canada's oldest ballet company. Here, the members of the company rehearse *Swan Lake.*

For fans of classical music, Canada has about thirty symphony orchestras. Young musicians between the ages of sixteen and twenty-eight can try out for the National Youth Orchestra, which tours Canada each summer. Many visitors to Canada's cities attend the opera or the ballet. Particularly prestigious is the Royal Winnipeg Ballet, which is one of the most highly regarded ballet companies in the world.

Art, Theater, and Film

Many cities feature museums that showcase the works of Canadian visual artists. Art enthusiasts can visit the extensive collections of the National Gallery of Canada in Ottawa and the Royal Ontario Museum in Toronto. The McMichael Canadian Art Collection in Kleinburg, Ontario, focuses exclusively on art made by Canadians, including works by First Nations and Inuit artists. In Quebec City, the National Museum of Fine Arts of Quebec celebrates the artistic traditions of the province of Quebec.

These museums, as well as many others throughout the world, display works of particularly notable Canadian artists, such as Paul Kane, Emily Carr, Agnes Martin, Bill Reid, and Norval Morrisseau. Canadians have also made important contributions to the world of literature. They include the novelists Douglas Coupland, Margaret Atwood, Robertson Davies, and

The Crystal, a new section of the Royal Ontario Museum in Toronto, opened in 2007.

Anne of Green Gables

Probably the most famous book by a Canadian author is *Anne of Green Gables*. Written by Lucy Maud Montgomery, it was first published in the United States in 1908. A Canadian edition did not appear until 1943. The book tells the story of an imaginative, high-spirited, redheaded orphan named Anne, who goes to live on Prince Edward Island. The book spawned seven sequels about Anne. Montgomery's books are still widely read around the world. They bring to Prince Edward Island a steady stream of tourists who want to see the world in which their beloved Anne lived.

Mordecai Richler. Each year, the government of Canada honors exceptional achievements in literature, the visual arts, and the performing arts with the Governor General's Awards.

Canada is also known for theater. After New York City, Toronto is the most vibrant theater center in North America. Its theaters present everything from big-budget musicals to small experimental productions. Stratford, Ontario, is also a popular destination for theater lovers. From May through November, the city hosts the Stratford Festival. The festival features the works of William Shakespeare, as well as other classic and contemporary plays. Dominating the French-speaking theater scene is Théâtre du Nouveau Monde (Theater of the New World), a company based in Montreal.

Most of the films shown in Canadian movie theaters are made in Hollywood. Only about 5 percent are produced by Canadian filmmakers. The government, however, has taken an active role in developing the Canadian film industry. Its National Film Board produces and distributes a wide variety of Canadian-made movies. The works of several Canadian movie directors, most notably David Cronenberg and Atom Egoyan, make regular appearances at film festivals throughout the world. Another famous figure in Canada's film industry is Denys Arcand. This French Canadian director is best known for his film *The Barbarian Invasions*, which won the Academy Award for Best Foreign Language Film in 2004. Many Canadian actors have also made it big in Hollywood, including Jim Carrey and Mike Myers.

Jim Carrey is one of Canada's most popular stars. As of 2010, his films had earned $2.3 billion at the box office.

Customers read newspapers while having breakfast at a café in Montreal.

Perhaps Canada's greatest contribution to the art of moviemaking is the annual Toronto International Film Festival, the second-largest film festival in the world. The event takes place over ten days in early September. Filmmakers travel to Toronto from around the world to show their movies. At each festival, more than 250 new movies are screened for crowds and critics.

In a nation as large as Canada, the news media has an important role to play. Through newspapers, television, and radio, Canadians, no matter where they are, can keep abreast of what is happening in every corner of their country.

Canada has two national newspapers—the *Globe and Mail* and the *National Post*, both published in Toronto. In addition, every major city has at least one daily paper. There is also a lively trade in newspapers for non-English speakers. In Toronto alone, about one hundred newspapers are available in the many different languages of recent immigrants. French speakers can get their news through a variety of publications, including *La Presse* and *Le Devoir*.

Many of the radio and television stations in Canada are operated by the Canadian Broadcasting Corporation (CBC). Founded in the 1930s, the CBC is funded by both the Canadian government and commercial advertising. The CBC offers programming in both English and French. It also runs Radio Canada International, a special radio service for native peoples. In addition to CBC programming, Canadians enjoy a variety of commercial radio and television operations, including CTV, the country's largest television network.

Many of the programs shown on Canadian television come from other countries, particularly the United States. But since the early 1970s, the Canadian government has required that a certain percentage of television programs must be from Canada. This law has made many more jobs available to Canadian television producers, writers, and performers.

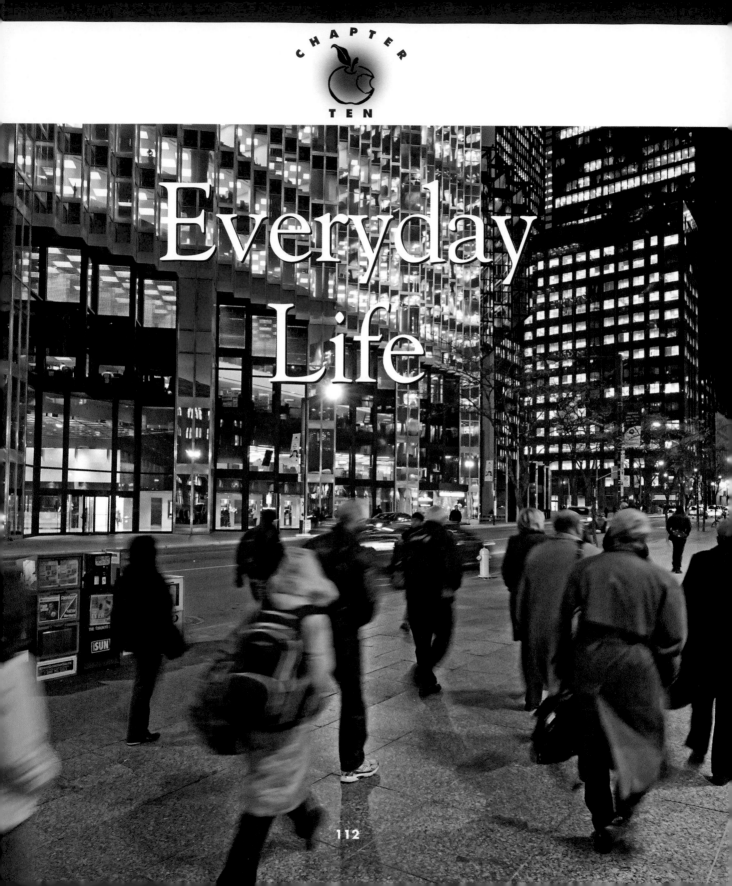

Everyday Life

In a country the size of Canada, how people live day to day depends on where they live. For instance, in rural areas of the Maritime Provinces, life moves at a relatively slow pace. People often have very close ties to their communities and tend to be open and friendly with their neighbors.

In contrast, many Canadians in large cities, such as Toronto, lead fast-paced lives. They often work in offices in the skyscrapers that dominate the downtown skyline. On nights and weekends, they are likely to scramble to take advantage of all their city has to offer—from fine restaurants to world-class museums to the hottest musical acts.

Still other areas in Canada have their own unique vibe. In Alberta, with its ranches and oil rigs, some people embrace a cowboy culture not too different from that in Texas. In British Columbia, people are known for their tolerant ways and embrace all things new. In Quebec, the French-inspired culture is apparent in everything from restaurant menus to street fashion. And in the northern territories, many Inuits spend much of their time hunting, fishing, and making artwork, just as their ancestors did long ago.

Opposite: **Some workers head to their offices in downtown Toronto before the sun is up.**

Snowsnakes

The Dene people of the Northwest Territories and Nunavut still play a traditional game called snowsnakes. The "snake" is a straight stick, about 4.5 feet (1.4 m) long, made from a spruce tree. The stick is sharpened at one end and varnished to create a slick surface. The players take turns sliding their sticks across a level field of packed ice. The player whose stick travels farthest wins. Every two years, teams of young players compete in snowsnakes and other Dene games at Canada's Arctic Winter Games.

Urban Living

Despite the differences among them, there are generalizations that can be made about typical Canadians and the way they live. Most Canadians are city dwellers. About four in five Canadians live in an urban area.

Many Canadian cities look more like European cities than American ones. Homes and shops are generally found in the same neighborhoods. Getting around is often easy by

Montreal has been voted one of the ten most bicycle-friendly cities in the world. It has more than 2,400 miles (3,900 km) of bike trails.

bike or on foot, which gives many areas, even in large cities, a comfortable neighborhood feel. Canadian houses are usually smaller than those in the United States. Row houses and small buildings with several homes are common.

Most Canadians live in the southern portion of the country. In fact, about 90 percent live within 125 miles (200 km) of Canada's border with the United States. Climate explains why the population of Canada is concentrated in the south. Large areas in the north are so cold that they have only scattered settlements. Although the three northern territories make up about one-third of the total area of Canada, only about three in every one thousand Canadians live there.

About 1,300 people live in Pond Inlet on Baffin Island. Most of them are Inuits.

The Sock Dance

In Quebec, some French Canadians indulge in a playful ritual as part of wedding receptions. The older unmarried brothers and sisters of the bride and groom take to the dance floor wearing the ugliest socks they can find. They then do a funny dance, while the wedding guests laugh and throw money at their feet. The money is given to the bride and groom to spend on their new household.

Education and Health

Canadians, as a rule, are well-educated. Some 99 percent can both read and write. Most children attend public schools that are operated by the provinces and territories. Three provinces—Ontario, Saskatchewan, and Alberta—offer students the chance to attend separate schools, which are public schools that teach classes from a religious perspective. Nearly all separate schools are for Catholics. Governments also fund both French-speaking and English-speaking schools. In Quebec, about 85 percent of students attend French-speaking schools.

Canadian students are required to attend school until at least age sixteen.

In most areas, students need to study twelve years to earn a high school diploma. (In Quebec, only eleven years are required.) After graduation, many students go on to one of Canada's many public and private universities. These include the University of Toronto, the University of Alberta, and McGill University. Major French-speaking universities include the University of Montreal, Laval University, and the University of Quebec.

Canadians also generally enjoy good access to health care. As a result, they have a high life expectancy—seventy-nine years for men and eighty-four years for women. Taxes pay for the national health care system, which is administered on the provincial and territorial level. Many people are proud of their health care system. In 2004, viewers of the television show *The Greatest Canadian* named Tommy Douglas, the politician most responsible for setting up their health care system, the greatest Canadian in history. The Canadian government has many other programs to help the poor and low-income workers. These programs and private charities help keep the poverty rate low in Canada.

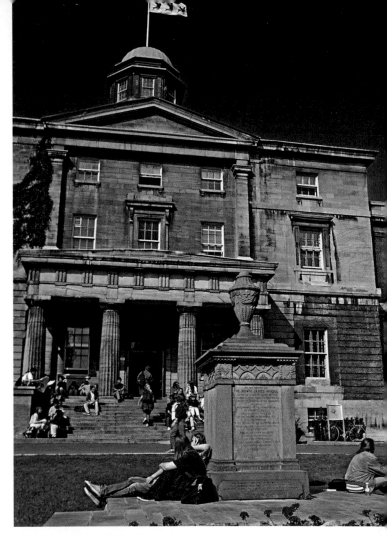

McGill University is generally considered the best university in Canada. It was founded in 1821.

A Sports-Loving Nation

Canadians are famed for their passion for watching sports. People across the nation were glued to their TVs the three times Canada hosted the Olympic Games. The Summer Olympics were held in Montreal in 1976, and the Winter Olympics were held in Calgary in 1988 and in Vancouver in 2010.

Name just about any sport, and Canadians follow it. The Toronto Raptors battle against leading American teams in the National Basketball Association. The Toronto Blue Jays, currently the only Major League Baseball team from outside the United States, won back-to-back World Series in 1992 and 1993. Since 2007, soccer fans have enjoyed games between the Edmonton Drillers, the Saskatoon Accelerators, and other teams of the Canadian Major Indoor Soccer League.

Fans celebrate the Canadian hockey team's gold medal victory over the United States during the 2010 Olympics in Vancouver.

Eight teams in Canada are members of the Canadian Football League. Canadian football is similar to American football, but there are a few differences. For example, Canadian teams field twelve players rather than eleven, and the size of their playing field is larger.

Despite Canadians' devotion to these teams, their greatest passion is ice hockey. Hockey is Canada's national pastime, and the sport was most likely a Canadian invention. It is said that the first game of ice hockey was played in Kingston, Ontario, in 1855.

Canadians everywhere follow the victories and defeats of the country's six teams in the National Hockey League—the

Hockey is the most popular sport in Canada. Many children learn to play when they are very young.

The Great Gretzky

Given Canada's obsession for hockey, it is hardly surprising that hockey star Wayne Gretzky is one of the most beloved Canadians of all time. Growing up in Brantford, Ontario, Gretzky learned to play the game on a backyard rink. When he was seventeen, he went professional, becoming the youngest athlete playing any major league sport in North America.

During his twenty-one-year career, he emerged as one of the greatest players ever. He was awarded the National Hockey League's Hart Memorial Trophy for most valuable player nine times. Gretzky's athletic talents and charisma excited not only Canadians. He also helped popularize the sport of hockey in the United States. Gretzky retired in 1999, but people still talk about the Great Gretzky.

Vancouver Canucks, Calgary Flames, Edmonton Oilers, Toronto Maple Leafs, Montreal Canadiens, and Ottawa Senators. Many of the greatest hockey stars of all time, including Wayne Gretzky and Guy Lafleur, played on Canadian teams.

For many families, *Hockey Night in Canada*, which began airing in 1952, is a Saturday night ritual. It has long been one of the highest-rated shows in Canada. Many Canadians jokingly call the show's famous theme song, used from 1968 to 2008, Canada's unofficial national anthem.

Many Canadians love to play hockey themselves, taking part in an amateur tournament or a pickup game on a frozen lake. Nearly half a million Canadians are enrolled as amateur players with the Canadian Hockey Association.

Stompin' Tom Connors

Canadian fans of the National Hockey League all know Stompin' Tom Connors. The singer-songwriter's 1992 hit, "The Hockey Song," is often played during games.

Born Charles Thomas Connors, Stompin' Tom began his professional singing career in 1964, playing at the Maple Leaf Hotel in Timmins, Ontario. To keep the rhythm amid the noisy audiences, he took to loudly stomping his foot—a habit that became his trademark and gave him his stage name. Popular on country music and university radio stations, Connors sings songs about Canadians and distinctly Canadian subjects. Militant about the need to support Canadian artists, in 1978 he famously returned his many Juno Awards, one of the most prestigious honors for the arts in Canada, because he claimed too many Junos were being given to Canadians who had moved out of the country.

For decades, Connors has enjoyed a large following. In 2000, he received the Governor General's Performing Arts Award. He has also inspired generations of Canadians to explore Canadian themes in music and art.

Nearly as beloved in Canada is lacrosse. In lacrosse, players use a stick with a net at one end to carry and pass a rubber ball. Teams score points by throwing the ball into a goal. A version of lacrosse was played by several First Nations groups before the arrival of Europeans in Canada. It has been popular there ever since.

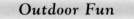

Outdoor Fun

No matter the season, Canadians look for ways to enjoy the great outdoors. When the weather is warm, cities are full of joggers and bicyclists. Other favorite summertime activities

Cross-country skiing and sledding are popular winter activities in Canada.

include hiking, swimming, and golfing. On weekends, many urban Canadians head out to small vacation homes in the country. Often, large families will gather at a country home to share their vacation together.

Even during the long winter, Canadians love outdoor sports. Many people don snowshoes and cross-country skis to make their way across snow-covered city parks. Others go sledding or ice-skating. Winnipeg claims the world's longest skating path. Located on the Assiniboine and Red Rivers, it stretches for more than 5 miles (8 km). Not to be outdone, Ottawa offers its residents the Rideau Canal, which, when it freezes over, becomes the world's largest ice-skating rink.

One of the most popular winter sports among Canadians is curling, in which two teams of four players slide granite stones along an ice-covered surface. The goal is to get the stones inside a target marked by a circle. The Canadian Curling Association estimates that there are more than one thousand curling clubs throughout the country. About one million Canadians participate in curling regularly.

As further proof of their love of the outdoors, many millions of Canadians make use of their country's extensive park system each year. The system is especially popular in July and August, when Canada's temperatures are at their highest. Every year, about sixteen million people visit the country's thirty-nine national parks. In addition, provincial and territorial governments operate more than one thousand parks of all types.

Backpackers head toward Russet Lake in British Columbia.

Poutine was first made in rural Quebec in the 1950s.

Eating Canadian

The day-to-day diet of Canadians is similar to that of Americans. In both countries, everyone enjoys the food from various immigrant groups. Especially in major urban areas, Canadians can easily dine out on delicacies from around the world.

There are, however, a few dishes that are closely associated with Canada. Most of these are commonly served in Quebec and reflect the French influence on that province. Perhaps the best known Canadian treat is *poutine*. This rich snack is made of French fries covered with gravy and cheese curds. The dish originated in Quebec, but it is now popular throughout Canada. Canadians also enjoy French fries sprinkled with malt vinegar.

Another Quebec delicacy is smoked meat. Montreal delicatessens are particularly known for this dish. Smoked meat is made of slices of beef brisket that has been soaked in spices and smoked.

French Canadians are famed, too, for their *tourtière*. This French-style meat pie, made from pork, veal, or beef, is a favorite part of the Christmas season for many Québécois.

Across Canada, the collection of sap from maple trees in the spring is cause for celebration. Canadians love visiting sugarhouses, where the sap is boiled into sugar. Traditionally, visitors to sugarhouses in Quebec sit down to a dinner of foods cooked in the sticky syrup. They might enjoy sausages, beans, eggs, or back bacon (also known as Canadian bacon), all infused with the sweet gift of the maple.

In the early spring, holes are drilled in maple trees, allowing the sap to run into buckets. The sap is used to make maple syrup.

Tim Hortons

In just about every populated area in Canada, you are likely to find a Tim Hortons nearby. Tim Hortons is the biggest fast-food chain in the country. It started as a single doughnut shop in Hamilton, Ontario, owned by hockey great Tim Horton, who died in a car accident in 1974. It has since grown to include more than three thousand locations in Canada and the United States.

Many Canadians think of the Tim Horton restaurants as a unique part of their culture. Local customers of "Timmies" have even added words and phrases to Canadian English. A *timbit* is a small dough ball, similar to what is called a doughnut hole in the United States. A *double-double* is a cup of coffee with two servings of sugar and cream.

Festivals and Holidays

Canadians look forward to many other annual festivals. In Alberta, one of the most exciting events each year is the Calgary Stampede, the world's largest rodeo. In August, Newfoundland and Labrador hosts the Royal St. John's Regatta. This annual boat race, which was first held in 1826, is the oldest sporting event in North America. Cold weather provides the occasion for many winter festivals throughout the country. Most notable is the Carnaval de Québec, which begins in January in Quebec City. Featuring outdoor dance parties, dogsled races, and ice sculpture competitions, it is the worlds' largest winter festival.

The Calgary Stampede attracts more than a million visitors each year. It is the world's biggest rodeo.

Canadians also look forward to an array of holiday celebrations held throughout the year. Many are observed only in particular provinces or territories. Manitoba's Louis Riel Day, held the third Monday of each February, honors the Métis activist. On June 21, the people of the Northwest Territories remember the contributions of native peoples to Canadian history and society on National Aboriginal Day. Three days later, La Fête nationale du Québec (also called St. Jean Baptiste Day) celebrates Quebec's unique history and culture.

Nine national holidays are observed in Canada, including New Year's Day, Thanksgiving Day, and Christmas Day. Canada Day, held every July 1, commemorates the day in 1867 when Canada became an independent nation. Friends and family gather to enjoy the summer warmth at open-air concerts and parades down their local streets. After nightfall, they come together for fireworks displays. Watching rockets explode in the sky, Canadians, from sea to sea, think about what they all share, no matter where they are from—their love for their vast and varied country, and their joy in the adventure of being Canadian.

Canadian National Holidays

New Year's Day	January 1
Good Friday	Friday before Easter
Victoria Day	Monday before May 25
Canada Day	July 1
Labour Day	First Monday in September
Thanksgiving Day	Second Monday in October
Remembrance Day	November 11
Christmas Day	December 25
Boxing Day	December 26

Timeline

Canadian History

The first people cross from Asia into North America.	**ca. 12,000 years ago**
Explorer John Cabot arrives in what is now the island of Newfoundland.	1497
Jacques Cartier explores the St. Lawrence River and claims the surrounding area for France.	1534
Samuel de Champlain establishes a French settlement at the site of what is now Quebec City.	1608
The British defeat the French in the French and Indian War and take over most French lands in North America.	1763
The Quebec Act allows Canadians of French descent to speak French and practice Roman Catholicism.	1774

World History

ca. 2500 BCE	Egyptians build the pyramids and the Sphinx in Giza.
ca. 563 BCE	The Buddha is born in India.
313 CE	The Roman emperor Constantine legalizes Christianity.
610	The Prophet Muhammad begins preaching a new religion called Islam.
1054	The Eastern (Orthodox) and Western (Roman Catholic) Churches break apart.
1095	The Crusades begin.
1215	King John seals the Magna Carta.
1300s	The Renaissance begins in Italy.
1347	The plague sweeps through Europe.
1453	Ottoman Turks capture Constantinople, conquering the Byzantine Empire.
1492	Columbus arrives in North America.
1500s	Reformers break away from the Catholic Church, and Protestantism is born.
1776	The U.S. Declaration of Independence is signed.
1789	The French Revolution begins.

Canadian History

The Dominion of Canada is created, uniting the provinces of Quebec, Ontario, Nova Scotia, and New Brunswick.	1867
Canada adds the provinces of Manitoba, British Columbia, and Prince Edward Island.	1870s
The transcontinental railroad is completed.	1885
Gold is discovered in the Klondike region.	1896
Saskatchewan and Alberta become Canadian provinces.	1905
Huge reserves of oil are discovered in Alberta.	1947
Newfoundland (now Newfoundland and Labrador) becomes a province of Canada.	1949
Canada adopts the maple leaf flag.	1965
Canada adopts its present constitution.	1982
Canada, the United States, and Mexico sign the North American Free Trade Agreement (NAFTA).	1994
A referendum calling for Quebec's independence from the rest of Canada is narrowly defeated.	1995
The territory of Nunavut is created.	1999
Vancouver, British Columbia, hosts the Winter Olympics.	2010

World History

1865	The American Civil War ends.
1879	The first practical lightbulb is invented.
1914	World War I begins.
1917	The Bolshevik Revolution brings communism to Russia.
1929	A worldwide economic depression begins.
1939	World War II begins.
1945	World War II ends.
1957	The Vietnam War begins.
1969	Humans land on the Moon.
1975	The Vietnam War ends.
1989	The Berlin Wall is torn down as communism crumbles in Eastern Europe.
1991	The Soviet Union breaks into separate states.
2001	Terrorists attack the World Trade Center in New York City and the Pentagon in Washington, D.C.
2004	A tsunami in the Indian Ocean destroys coastlines in Africa, India, and Southeast Asia.
2008	The United States elects its first African American president.

Fast Facts

Official name: Canada

Capital: Ottawa

Official languages: English and French

Ottawa

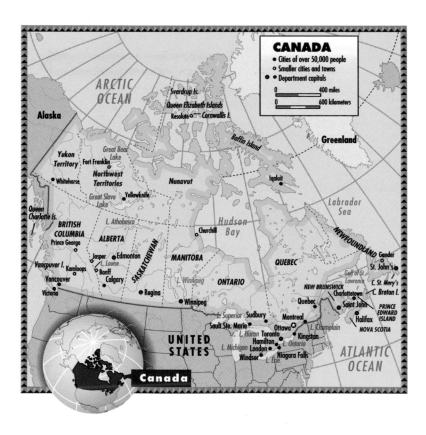

CANADA
- Cities of over 50,000 people
- Smaller cities and towns
- Department capitals

0   400 miles
0   600 kilometers

ARCTIC OCEAN

Alaska

Sverdrup Is.

Queen Elizabeth Islands

Resolute • Cornwallis I.

Baffin Island

Greenland

Yukon Territory

Fort Franklin

Great Bear Lake

Northwest Territories

Whitehorse

Nunavut

Iqaluit

Great Slave Lake

Yellowknife

Labrador Sea

Queen Charlotte Is.

BRITISH COLUMBIA

Prince George

L. Athabasca

ALBERTA

Churchill

Hudson Bay

NEWFOUNDLAND

Gander

Vancouver I.   Kamloops

Jasper

L. Louise

Edmonton

SASKATCHEWAN

MANITOBA

QUEBEC

St. John's

Vancouver

Banff

Calgary

L. Winnipeg

ONTARIO

Gulf of St. Lawrence

C. St. Mary's

Victoria

Regina

Winnipeg

NEW BRUNSWICK

Charlottetown

C. Breton I.

L. Superior   Sudbury

Quebec

Saint John

PRINCE EDWARD ISLAND

Sault Ste. Marie

Montreal

Halifax

UNITED STATES

L. Huron   Toronto

Ottawa

L. Champlain

Kingston

NOVA SCOTIA

Hamilton

L. Ontario

L. Michigan   London

Windsor

Niagara Falls

L. Erie

ATLANTIC OCEAN

Canada

Canadian flag

Official religion:	None
Year of founding:	1867
National anthem:	"O Canada"
Type of government:	Parliamentary democracy and confederation
Chief of state:	British monarch represented by governor general
Head of government:	Prime minister
Area:	3,855,102 square miles (9,984,668 sq km)
Latitude and longitude of geographic center:	60° N, 95° W
Bordering countries:	United States to the south and west
Highest elevation:	19,551 feet (5,959 m) at Mount Logan
Lowest elevation:	Sea level, along the coasts
Longest river:	Mackenzie River, 2,635 miles (4,241 km)

Saint Elias Range

CN Tower

Currency

National population (2006): 31,612,897

Population of largest cities (2006): Toronto, 2,503,281
Montreal, 1,620,693
Calgary, 988,193
Ottawa, 812,129
Edmonton, 730,372

Famous landmarks:
- ▶ *Big Nickel,* Sudbury, Ontario
- ▶ *Canada Olympic Park,* Calgary
- ▶ *CN Tower,* Toronto
- ▶ *Confederation Bridge,* connecting Prince Edward Island and New Brunswick
- ▶ *National Gallery,* Ottawa

Economy: Canada has one of the largest economies in the world. Manufacturing and mining are important, although the service sector has grown rapidly in recent years. Major goods produced in Canada include cars, lumber, machinery, iron ore, and aluminum. Canada is also a leading producer of energy, including oil, natural gas, and hydroelectric power. Some of Canada's most important agricultural products are wheat, barley, and beef. Its largest trading partner is the United States, which purchases about three-fourths of all Canadian exports.

Currency: The Canadian dollar. In 2011, 1.00 Canadian dollar was worth 1.03 U.S. dollars.

System of weights and measures: Metric system

Literacy rate: 99%

Students

Celine Dion

Common Canadian words and phrases:

First Nations	Native groups known as Native Americans in the United States
loonie	A one-dollar Canadian coin
Métis	Canadians of mixed First Nations and European ancestry
poutine	French fries topped with cheese curds and gravy
Québécois	French-speaking residents of Quebec
toonie	A two-dollar Canadian coin

Prominent Canadians:

Celine Dion *Singer*	(1968–)
Terry Fox *Activist*	(1958–1981)
Wayne Gretzky *Hockey player*	(1961–)
Lucy Maud Montgomery *Author*	(1874–1942)
Louis Riel *Rebel leader*	(1844–1885)
Pierre Trudeau *Prime minister*	(1919–2000)

To Find Out More

Books

▶ Moore, Christopher. *The Big Book of Canada: Exploring the Provinces and Territories*. Plattsburgh, NY: Tundra Books, 2002.

▶ Sakany, Lois. *Canada: A Primary Source Cultural Guide*. New York: Rosen Publishing, 2004.

▶ Williams, Brian. *Canada*. Washington, DC: National Geographic, 2009.

Web Sites

▶ **Atlas Canada**
http://atlas.nrcan.gc.ca/site/english
For reference maps of Canada.

▶ **Canadian Encyclopedia**
www.thecanadianencyclopedia.com
For articles on all subjects written from a Canadian point of view.

▶ **Dictionary of Canadian Biography Online**
www.biographi.ca
For biographies of prominent Canadians.

▶ **Government of Canada**
www.gc.ca
For information and news about the Canadian government.

▶ **Statistics Canada**
www.statcan.gc.ca
For statistics and data about Canada's economy and its people.

Embassies

▶ **Embassy of Canada**
501 Pennsylvania Avenue NW
Washington, DC 20001
202/682-1740
www.canadainternational.gc.ca
/washington/index.aspx?lang=eng

▶ **Canadian Consulate General**
1251 Avenue of the Americas
New York, NY 10020
212/596-1628
www.canadainternational.gc.ca
/new_york/index.aspx?lang=eng

Index

Page numbers in *italics*
indicate illustrations.

education and, 94, 116
government and, 94, 101
Islam, 93, 98–99, *98*
Judaism, 93, 97, *97*
kirpan (ceremonial sword), 100, *100*
native people, 93–94, 100–101, *101*
nonreligious population, 93, 100
Notre-Dame Basilica, *92*
potlatch ceremony, 101, *101*
Protestantism, 93, 95–96, *95*
Quebec Act of 1774, 49
Sikhism, 99, *99*, 100, *100*
St. Joseph's Oratory of Mount Royal, *94*
synagogues, 97, *97*
United Church of Canada, 93, 95–96
Remembrance Day, 55, 127
reptilian life, 33–34
Richler, Mordecai, 107–108
Riel, Louis, 53, *53*, 127, 133
Roberts, Edward, 68
Routhier, Adolphe-Basile, 64
Royal Ontario Museum, 23, 106–107, *107*
Royal St. John's Regatta, 126
Royal Winnipeg Ballet, 106, *106*

S
Saint Elias mountains, 24–25, *24*
Saskatchewan, 24, 51, 52, 53, 75, 81, 96, 116
Saskatoon, 24
Senate, 62, 67
service industries, 79–80, *80*
Sikhism, 99, *99*, 100, *100*
skiing, 23, 122, *122*
snowshoe hares, 37
snowsnakes game, 114
soccer, 118

sports, 13, *13*, 23, 40, 81, *81*, *91*, 114, 118–121, *118*, *119*, *120*, 121–123, *122*, *123*, 126, *126*
Stadacona (Iroquois village), 45
St. Jean Baptiste Day, 127
St. Joseph's Oratory of Mount Royal, *94*
St. Lawrence Lowlands. *See* Great Lakes-St. Lawrence Lowlands.
St. Lawrence River, 23, 27, *44*, 45
St. Lawrence Seaway, 27
Stratford Festival, 108
Supreme Court of Canada, 64, 66, 100
Szilva, Ted, 75

T
Tax Court of Canada, 66
television, 14, 111, 120
territories
    Northwest Territories, 20, 27, 41, 51–52, 69, 74, 87, 88, 114, 127
    Nunavut Territory, 51–52, 69, 81, 87, 88, *88*, 114
    Yukon Territory, 24, 34, 51, 52, 69, 87
Terry Fox Run, 14, *15*
theater, 108
Théâtre du Nouveau Monde (Theater of the New World), 108
Thunder Bay, *17*
Tim Hortons restaurants, 126
toonies (currency), 76
Toronto (provincial capital), *14*, 22, 23, *23*, 28, 29, 80, 83, 88, 97, *97*, 99, 103, 107, *107*, 108, 110, 111, *112*, 113
Toronto Blue Jays (baseball team), 118
Toronto International Film Festival, 110
Toronto Raptors (basketball team), 118

totem poles, 86
tourism, 80–81, *81*, 108
tourtière (meat pie), 125
Trans-Canada Highway, 79
transcontinental railroad, 53
transportation, 27, *27*, 52, 53, 78–79, *78*, 87, 88, *114*
Trudeau, Pierre, 13, 14, 61, *61*, 133

U
United Church of Canada, 93, 95–96

V
Vancouver, 80, 82, 88, 97, 100, 118, *118*
Vancouver Island, 25, 29, 36
Varley, Frederick, 103
Victoria, 8, 60, 79
Victoria, queen of England, 60, 65
Vikings, 43

W
water sports, 40
West Edmonton Mall, 80
whales, 36, *36*
wildlife. *See* amphibian life; animal life; insect life; marine life; plant life; reptilian life.
Winnipeg, 24, 122
Witless Bay Ecological Reserve, *35*, 41
Wolfe, James P., 48
wolves, 38
Wood Buffalo National Park, 41
World War I, 54–55
World War II, 55–56

Y
Yellowknife, 20
Yukon Territory, 24, 34, 51, 52, 69, 87

Meet the Author

A GRADUATE OF SWARTHMORE COLLEGE, Liz Sonneborn is a full-time writer living in Brooklyn, New York. She has written more than eighty nonfiction books for children and adults on a wide variety of subjects. Her books include *The American West*, *A to Z of American Indian Women*, *The Ancient Kushites*, *The Vietnamese Americans*, *Chronology of American Indian History*, *Guglielmo Marconi*, and *The Environmental Movement*.

Sonneborn was excited to take on a book about Canada for the best reason a writer ever gets: to be paid for studying and writing about a subject she was already very interested in. She says, "For many years, I've studied the history of native peoples in North America, the battle between the French and British for control of the continent, and the later struggles between various forces in the frontier West. This project was a chance to delve into all those subjects, but from a different perspective, from a Canadian perspective." It was also an opportunity to learn more about the modern nation of Canada. Sonneborn explains, "Like many, if not most Americans, I frequently take our northern neighbors for granted. But Canada, in the past and the present, is an amazing place. I'm so happy to have had an opportunity to learn and reflect about that."

Previously, Sonneborn had written about the United Arab Emirates and Yemen for the Enchantment of the World series. Those two books presented the same research challenge: a limited number of available sources in English. Researching Canada could not have been more different. "There are so many terrific sources, it was difficult choosing the best ones," Sonneborn explains. "I decided to focus on articles and books written by Canadian authors. I also relied heavily on online information provided by the government of Canada. For readers interested in learning more about Canada, I would recommend the online Canadian Encyclopedia (www.the canadianencyclopedia.com). It is an excellent resource."

Sonneborn has visited Canada numerous times. Close to home, she has found a way to reintroduce herself to Canadian culture—through her stomach. Near her Brooklyn neighborhood, a Montreal-style deli has opened to much acclaim. Purely for research purposes, of course, she indulged in plates of smoked meat and poutine, which she is happy to report, were fabulous. She also made her way to Brooklyn's only Tim Hortons, Canada's famed fast-food chain. There, a lovely doughnut and coffee gave her more welcome insights into all things Canadian.

Photo Credits

age fotostock: 40 (Donald C. & Priscilla/ Lonely Planet Images), back cover (FB-Rose/imagebroker), 80 (Jeff Greenberg), 97 (Oleksiy Maksymenko/ All Canada Photos), 81 (Stuart Westmorland);

Alamy Images: 89 (Aurora Photos), 39 (Steve Bloom Images), 112 (William Brooks), 122 (Bill Brooks), 21 (Will Burwell), 108 (Danita Delimont), 116, 133 top (First Light), 110 (Jeff Greenberg), 17 (Bert Hoferichter), 102 (Marshall Ikonography), 82 (Gunter Marx), 90, 114, 119 (Megapress), 18 (David Noton Photography), 26 (Thomas Peter Widmann/LOOK Die Bildagentur der Fotografen GmbH), 55 (Norman Pogson), 100 (Boaz Rottem), 99 (Andrew Rubtsov), 84 (David Sanger Photography), 88 (tbkmedia.de), 106 (WorldFoto), 115 (Konrad Wothe/LOOK Die Bildagentur der Fotografen GmbH);

AP Images: 95 (Amber Bracken, Edmonton Sun via The Canadian Press), 121 (Frank Gunn, The Canadian Press), 105, 133 bottom (Julie Jacobson), 50 (North Wind Picture Archives), 98 (Ryan Remiorz, The Canadian Press), 104 (Steffen Schmidt/Keystone), 63 (Adrian Wyld/ The Canadian Press), 120;

Corbis Images/Gary Hershorn/Reuters: 61;

Dreamstime.com: 91 (Serguei Bachlakov), 107 (Gary Blakeley), 70 (Kelly Boreson), 60 (Alexandre Fagundes De Fagundes), 22 (Robert Fraser), 127 (Lijuan Guo), 92 (Jun He), 65 right, 130 left (Leo Bruce Hempell), 66, 76, 132 bottom (Ken Pilon), 58 (Seregal), 34 bottom (Thomas Smith), 8 (Sumeet Wadhwa);

Getty Images: 94 (Rogerio Barbosa/AFP), 75 (Norm Betts/Bloomberg), 124 (David Boily/AFP), 86 (Lynn Johnson/National Geographic), 30 (Don Johnston/All Canada Photos), 109 (George Pimentel/ WireImage), 118 (Mark Ralston/AFP), 2 (George Rose), 101 (Ted Spiegel/National Geographic);

Inmagine: 67, 131 top;

iStockphoto/Orchidpoet: 32;

Landov, LLC/Reuters: 77 (Mark Blinch), 68 (Chris Wattie);

Liz Sonneborn: 143;

Media Bakery: 16 (LWA/Dann Tardif), 11 (Steve Smith);

NEWSCOM: 12 (Boris Spremo/Toronto Star/ZUMA Press), 15 (SUN), 13 (t14/ ZUMA Press), 14 (Toronto Star/ZUMA Press);

Robert Fried Photography: cover, 6, 117;

ShutterStock, Inc.: 35 (Chris Alcock), 33 (John Czenke), 29 (Elena Elisseeva), 126 (Steve Estvanik), 56 (Stephen Finn), 34 top (Brian Lasenby), 37, 78, 123 (David P. Lewis), 36, 38 (Mayskyphoto), 125 (Norman Pogson);

Superstock, Inc.: 72, 79 (All Canada Photos), 23, 132 top (Robert Harding Picture Library), 7 top, 27 (Wolfgang Kaehler), 24, 25, 131 bottom (Minden Pictures), 7 bottom, 41 (NaturePL), 87 (NHPA), 42 (The Art Archive);

The Granger Collection, New York: 47 (Henri Beau), 44 (J.A.T. Gudin), 54 (Sydney Prior Hall), 48 (Augustus Tholey), 46, 51 bottom, 52, 53;

The Image Works/Roger-Viollet: 96.

Maps by XNR Productions, Inc.